THE VICTORIAN HOUSE

John Marshall & Ian Willox

The Victorian House

SIDGWICK & JACKSON, LONDON
in association with Channel Four Television Company Limited

First published in Great Britain in October 1986
by Sidgwick & Jackson Limited
1 Tavistock Chambers, Bloomsbury Way
London WC1A 2SG

Reprinted April 1987

Designed by James Campus

ISBN 0–283–99363–4

Phototypeset by Falcon Graphic Art Ltd
Wallington, Surrey
Printed and bound by Butler & Tanner
Frome, Somerset

PICTURE ACKNOWLEDGEMENTS

B.T. Batsford 132
Bridgeman Art Library 62 *right*, 70, 125 *above and below*, 129
   right
James Campus 88, 107
Mary Evans Picture Library 8, 10 *above*, 13, 18 *below*, 22, 29,
   32, 44, 68, 77, 86, 96, 101, 103 *below*, 106, 108, 126, 133
   left and right
Fotomas Index 9, 12, 18 *above*, 30 *above*, 48, 71, 72, 74, 85,
   99
C.P. Hart 135
Illustrated London News Picture Library 10 *below*, 16, 30
   below, 40, 62 *left*, 84, 91, 113 *right*, 117
K. Jagger 54, 56, 100, 112, 138, 142, 143, 144, 148, 157
Peter Keen F R S A 52, 122
Kensington Public Library 36, 67
London Architectural Salvage and Supply Co. Ltd 153 *above,
   below left and below right*
London Borough of Hackney 43, 66, 79, 102, 103 *above*
London Borough of Wandsworth 19, 160
Mansell Collection 14, 15, 17, 20, 24, 25, 27, 65, 115, 162
   above and below
John Marshall 34, 46, 49, 93, 95, 97, 110, 141, 146, 150 *left
   and right*
Museum of Labour History 33
National Buildings Record 111
National Trust 119, 131
Science Museum, London 83 (Bridgeman Art Library), 87
Sidgwick and Jackson Archives 78, 113 *left*
Victoria and Albert Museum, London 26, 61, 73, 90, 92, 121,
   156 *above and below*, 158, 159, 164
Victorian Society 64
Whitworth Art Gallery, Manchester (Bridgeman Art Library)
   129 *left*
Christopher Wood 59

Architectural drawings on pages 39 and 51 by Henryk Lach of
   Tectiform
Picture research by Mary Jane Coles

CONTENTS

ACKNOWLEDGEMENTS vi

INTRODUCTION vii

1. Where Do Victorian Houses Come From? 9

2. How They Were Built 32

3. The Home Within 57

4. Exteriors, Gardens and Beyond 92

5. A Home Fit for Living 120

6. A Buyer's Guide 140

7. History of Your House 155

FURTHER READING 165

USEFUL ADDRESSES 167

INDEX 172

ACKNOWLEDGEMENTS

There are many people who helped in the compilation of this book to whom thanks are due: Charles Brooking, for his advice and access to his collection of windows and architectural furnishings; Victor Belcher and Frank Kelsall of the former GLC Historic Buildings Division, for their expertise; Charles Wainwright and Francis Collard at the Victoria and Albert Museum, for their guidance; John Fidler, Louise Snell and Dr Thacker of the Historic Buildings and Monuments Commission, for their enthusiasm; Tim Foster, for educating us in elementary architecture; Julian Harrup, for introducing us to the complexities of architecture; Ian Grant, for revealing our ignorance; Rosemarie MacQueen and Mike Lownes in the Planning Department of the London Borough of Hackney, for patiently unknotting the complex and fast-changing world of house planning; Helen Long, for her knowledge of interiors; and, finally, Andrew Patterson and Henryk Lach of Tectiform, for supplying and checking many of the practical details of the book. What is good in this book is thanks to them; the mistakes are ours alone.

INTRODUCTION

One-third of the houses in Britain were built before the First World War, and the huge majority of them are Victorian. They are the houses in which many of us live but, more than that, they still characterize our cities and set a standard for what we expect a house to be. Strictly speaking, a Victorian house is one constructed during the reign of the Queen, from 1837 to 1901, but the methods and materials that Victorian builders employed can frequently be found in earlier, Georgian and Regency, buildings and in those originating in the years up to 1914. Apart from superficially different decorative embellishments, the Victorian house remained basically unchanged throughout the period. What did change were materials – brick, slate and glass became nationally available through the development of the railway system and the growth of technology.

It is estimated that close to six million Victorian houses were built. A time of rapid population growth and the expansion of the cities, it produced a huge demand for housing. This was met through the work of thousands of small speculative builders, each constructing perhaps only a few houses and many of them succumbing to the economic pressures that this entailed. Yet most of their houses still stand today and have been lived in by generations of people seeking a sturdy home and a front door to close against the world outside. These builders were the real heroes behind the houses. Most of them would not know an architect if they saw one, and their work was based on practical experience. If they were conservative in their designs it was because they knew they were building for a market which rarely appreciated the different or the avant-garde – bankruptcy was close enough to the spec builder without the need to take risks.

This book looks at the product of their labours and enterprise, at the way the houses were decorated and furnished, and at the society which produced them. Informed Victorian circles worried greatly about the lack of an original architectural style that they could call their own, a truly 'Victorian' style. While they discussed the point, the builders got on with it, creating what we can now recognize as the Victorian house and which, increasingly, is regarded as a human model for housing in the future, especially after the follies of the tower blocks of the fifties and sixties.

Technological change and social transformation in the nineteenth century combined to produce a period which was in many respects chaotic – the belief that tomorrow really would be different was based not in empty philosophy but in the everyday experience of ordinary people. Low life expectancy resulted in the rapid movement of inherited wealth, while speculative ventures meant that fortunes were as easily lost as found. The constant presence of sickness and ill health demanded both respect for the after-life and a belief that one should live for today while building for the future.

Through their energy and drive the Victorians shaped the cities and industries we have inherited, just as we have inherited their houses. But, in addition, something less tangible has been passed down to us – the idea of home, of a place where, at the end of our working day, we can lead the life we choose behind the bay window of its façade. These homes, more than the grand houses or the monumental public buildings, represent the essence of Britain, and they should not be ignored simply because they surround us in our daily lives. The Victorian house is a symbol of Britain itself. It is something to be proud of, which we should celebrate and enjoy.

John Marshall
Ian Willox

'I painted the washstand in the servant's bedroom,' wrote the ardent self-improver Mr Pooter in *The Diary of a Nobody* whilst in the thrall of a pot of red enamel.

1. Where Do Victorian Houses Come From?

London going out of Town or The March of Bricks & Mortar, an engraving by George Cruikshank, 1829. The beginnings of urban sprawl.

The Victorian house and home were the result of a massive increase in the urban population during the nineteenth century. In the first half of that century the population of Britain increased from nine to eighteen million and kept on growing. This growth was paralleled by the great shift of the population away from the countryside and towards the towns and cities, swelling them to bursting point. At the start of the century only 20 per cent of the British population lived in cities; by 1851 those cities contained 54 per cent. Cities have always exerted a fascination over the ambitious country dweller, but this huge movement of people was rather more than that. The first major wave of the industrial revolution, heralded by the railways, had made the towns and cities its focus. Materials could be transported to the factory, instead of the factory going to the raw materials. Once a factory was established, workers

Belgrave Square, London: thoroughly Georgian. The fashionable estates built in cities in Georgian and Regency days were the forerunners of the more modest Victorian terraces in more distant suburbs.

An artist's impression of working men's dwellings on a new estate being put up in the 1870s. On the far right are stacks of bricks and timber for houses still to be constructed, and a railway line runs past the back of the houses on the left.

were needed, and they in turn needed food, clothing, housing and entertainment, which attracted yet more people and commercial enterprises to the towns and cities. Goods and people began to be centralized in a way that would have been impossible without the railways. It was a vicious circle: rural life and work on the land declined, forcing yet more people into the cities in search of better opportunities. Many ended up in the rookeries and slums that were to become a familiar landmark of the industrial revolution and Victorian England, but others made successful lives for themselves.

It was one thing to make a living in these newly important cities, but quite another to find somewhere to live. The problem was even worse than in today's crowded cities. Modern cities can at least expand to cope with their population, because they now have the transport systems to enable people to commute. The average Victorian city-dweller walked to work, and therefore his home had to be within walking distance of his job – two or three miles was normal; few could afford a cab or carriage, and buses and trams had not yet been introduced. Gradually the first suburbs began to develop, straining at the edges of walking distance from the areas where people worked. The people who moved there tended to be in lower middle-class occupations – clerks and the like – whose salary kept them in the middle classes purely by dint of extremely careful management of resources. Accommodation of a standard they considered appropriate to their class was almost unaffordable in town; most of the property within their price range was too close to the slums in both proximity and nature. So they were faced with a simple choice – starve for the sake of a decent address, or find somewhere cheaper further afield. These clerks, in their top hats and tailcoats, could be seen solemnly walking to and from work in the City and in the counting houses at the beginning and end of each working day. This was the first real impetus towards suburban development, but it made no significant impact on the huge and growing problem. Space for housing lay all around the cities – the trouble was getting to and from that space.

The railways which had helped bring about the problem of urban over-population were of very little help initially. Railway engineers were still solving the problems of laying rails across the countryside, quite often in the teeth of resistance from local landowners. They had neither the energy nor the money to force a passage through to the centre of a densely built city, which would require the wholesale eviction of thousands of families and the destruction of their homes. By the late nineteenth century all this would have changed. A network of railways would have been better established, enabling commuter suburbs to go up in places as far away as Penge and Enfield. In the early part of

Victoria's reign, though the railway could take you to the city, it only went as far as the edge. You had to make your own way to the centre.

In 1837, however, a line was laid from Deptford and Bermondsey in the East End to London Bridge, the first terminus anywhere near a useful part of the City of London. The route was already served by an existing stagecoach and steamboat, both of whom the London and Greenwich Railway Company hoped to undercut – even offering a third-class ticket for passengers who did not mind standing. But despite being cheaper and quicker than stage and boat, the railway was doomed to failure. It was designed to carry commuters, but there were no commuters. The London and Greenwich ran their rails through country that was mostly uninhabited – there were no houses for would-be commuters to live in. A steamboat down the Thames was a favourite holiday pastime, and soon the railway found that most of their passengers were day trippers at the weekends and on public holidays. Their quietest times were during the working week – the very time they had banked on being their busiest and most lucrative. This was, however, the first railway line to express any interest in commuters, and it did establish a bridgehead near the centre of London. It had sidestepped the problem that faced every railway company wanting to get to the heart of the city – the problem of cutting through thousands of houses – by taking the line of least resistance into London. What the company had gained by choosing an unpopulated route they lost by running an unpopular one. But their failure paved the way for the others' success.

Euston Arch, Euston Station, London, c. 1890. The cabs are waiting to take commuters to their final destination.

Below: The construction of a cutting at Camden Town for the London end of the London to Birmingham Railway. The nomadic navvies who built the railways and the canals got twice the wage of ordinary labourers. They were not popular with local inhabitants, despite their spendthrift ways, because of their numbers, their strength and their lawless disposition.

Railways were kept at bay in North London, mainly by the powerful interests of the West End and the City who ensured that the cost of acquiring sites rose alarmingly the nearer they were to the centre. So the London railway network terminated in a series of stations arranged around the fringes of the city – Euston (1837) and Kings Cross (1852) in the north, and Paddington (1854) in the west, began to balance London Bridge in the south. But even at this distance from the centre these new lines cut chasms through whole districts, eliminating vast stretches of housing and making many homeless. To keep down their costs the railways built their lines through the poorest areas, where housing was cheapest and resistance most easily overcome. Sometimes they would even build over the roads and houses, using brick arches; the vacant spaces under the arches were let as warehouses and sometimes even as

Doré's engraving gives an idea of the appallingly overcrowded and oppressed living conditions of a mid-Victorian city, which the railways did nothing to improve.

accommodation. It was little compensation for the eighty thousand Londoners displaced by railways between 1853 and 1900.

This displacement by development was nothing new in the nineteenth century; indeed, it was regarded as an honourable method of social engineering. If the developers had to drive a road through the city, then better to drive it through the slums, they considered, because in this way they not only kept the cost of land purchase down but also eliminated the slum; they never worried about where the dispossessed ended up. New Oxford Street, for example, built in 1841, cut through a notorious rookery, Church Lane.

The term 'rookery' describes rather more than a simple slum. The ingrowth of Victorian cities created slums in the no man's land between estates where every available space was colonized, creating a maze of human nests and burrows made more noisome by open cess-trenches and rubbish tips. They were a nexus of disease, crime and poverty. In place of streets there were tiny paths, tunnels and runways accessible only to the denizens of the rookery. As Kellow Chesney wrote in *The Victorian Underworld*, it was the haunt of 'whores, pandars, crimps, bullies and catamites', concealed, as often as not, in the shadows of the homes of the rich and powerful. It is easy to understand the Victorians' desire to raze such places to the ground, yet sometimes they defeated their own ends. Some of the Church Lane rookery's buildings still survive, though now renamed Bucknall Street; the remainder disappeared in the construction of New Oxford Street. Before the new road was built there were 27 houses in Church Lane, inhabited by 655 persons. By 1847, six years

The remains of the notorious slum called Church Lane, seen here in an 1870s' print, survived over a century of urban improvements to become a quiet backwater amidst the bustle of Bloomsbury traffic, in the shadow of Centre Point.

CHURCH LANE
BLOOMSBURY

later, because of the blight brought about by New Oxford Street those same houses contained no fewer than 1095 human beings – mostly refugees from demolished slums. By attacking the symptoms of overcrowding, the planners made the diseases of overcrowding much, much worse.

The new railway termini in London made many homeless, brought more people to the inner city and had little or no effect on the development of commuter traffic; indeed the railway companies showed very little interest in it. The infrastructure of trams and buses that allowed the less well-heeled commuter arriving by train to get to his final destination was late in developing. Until that time, commuting remained an expensive minority habit. The commuters who did start to use the railway networks tended to be the better off ones anyway, since the high cost of a railway ticket effectively excluded the working classes. The main effect of the arrival of railways in town was a huge increase in the demand for horses, since both the passengers and the goods that the railways brought needed to be taken on from the terminus.

The first hint of improvement came with the introduction of the horse-drawn omnibus, a Parisian invention which had first been brought to London by Mr George Shillibeer in 1829. It was not so much a technological invention as a conceptual one. The omnibus was very similar to a stagecoach and not unlike the 'short stage' which operated in and around London, but its selling point was its ability to carry a lot of passengers – up to fifteen – along a pre-arranged

By 1855 some 20,000 people used the horse-drawn omnibus every day in London. This one, De Tivoli's patent omnibus, introduced to London in 1860, ran from Paddington to London Bridge. It had provision for four second-class passengers on top but was still too expensive for many working men.

Kennington Gate Turnpike, London – an engraving of 1865, just about the time it was removed. The street sweeper in the foreground is trying to make some impression on the mire.

route through town with frequent stops. It should have filled the gap between cabs and stagecoaches; instead it was squeezed out between them. The omnibus was slower than the short stagecoach. It also had to compete with the hackney cab drivers who had a monopoly of public transport within the square mile of the City of London. The omnibuses also turned out to be too wide for narrow city streets. George Shillibeer went bankrupt.

Nevertheless his idea bore fruit, firstly in the abolition of the hackney cab monopoly in the City, and secondly in the bus mania that gripped Britain. As the companies vied for routes and passengers, the network of stops and schedules evolved until they were usable by the commuter. Competition kept the fares down, though the turnpikes through which the buses had to pass not only slowed down the services but also raised the price of tickets again. A letter to *The Times* in 1850 complained that the new tolls in Peckham had put up the fare to town by a penny – no small sum in those days. To be fair, the turnpikes had been hard hit by the shift of long-distance traffic from the roads to the railways, and were desperate to exact tolls where they could. But it meant that fares were high and only a small section of the population could afford to use a bus as a regular way of getting to work.

THE IMPROVED STREET RAILWAY CARRIAGE.
PATENTED BY GEORGE FRANCIS TRAIN.

Left above: George Francis Train's tram, *c.* 1861: finally a form of transport that almost everyone could afford.

Left below: A test ride on the Paddington to Farringdon Street line, 1862, now a major segment of the Circle and Metropolitan line in London's underground system. Ventilation on the early underground was a major problem – the fumes from the engine often nearly asphyxiated passengers.

It was not until the second railway boom, in the 1860s, that commuting really took hold of the working population. The congestion in inner London had now got so bad that in 1863 the first underground railway had to be built, between Paddington and Farringdon Street. The middle classes who could afford to commute were safe in their villas and terraces, while the working classes were trapped in the centre of the city. The time was ripe for change, and an American by the unlikely name of George Train thought that he had the answer: in 1861 he introduced the horse-drawn tram to London. But the rails he laid for his trams caused howls of outrage from the carriage-owning classes, who claimed that they interfered with their vehicles. The rails and the trams had to be scrapped. Like Shillibeer and his ill-fated omnibus, it was a failure, but also a sign of things to come.

By the end of the next decade there was a network of trams operating in London. In the city centre itself, trams were excluded by buses in much the same way that hackney cabs had kept out the early buses. Trams were strongest in the suburbs just outside the centre. It is said that Whitehorse Lane in Thornton Heath, South London, took its name from the horse that was kept as a standby to help pull the trams up that particular hill. The virtues of trams were their cheapness and regularity. They also ran at times which suited the

One of the omnibuses that rapidly supplied an efficient transport network for south London, fare one penny.

working-class population, and they offered cheap fares for those workers. The effect was dramatic. Finally the working classes could follow the middle classes in their flight to the suburbs. 'We have relieved London of an immense number of poor people by carrying them out to the suburbs,' said a jubilant chairman of London Tramways. His trams complemented the changing policy of the suburban railway companies.

It had been in the interest of the estate developers in the suburbs to try to keep them as exclusive as possible. To this end they used various means to encourage the railways – who were often the developer anyway – to offer only first-class fares to their suburban stations and to prevent trains that might be carrying working men from stopping at them. But now it dawned on both developers and railways that there was a growing demand for working-class housing in the suburbs. Encouraged by developers, the railway companies introduced ticket systems of byzantine complexity, designed to ensure that working-class passengers were conveyed to their destinations in the suburbs,

Arrival of the workmen's penny train at Victoria Station.

and the middle classes to theirs, without their paths crossing and without their having to share a station platform. It is some indication of the willingness of railway companies to offer these advantages to the working classes that as late as 1883 an Act of Parliament was required to make it obligatory for railway companies to offer a working man's fare. The effects of this release of the working classes from the bondage of inner cities can be best seen in London, where the working-class suburb of Willesden grew from a mere 3000 inhabitants in 1851 to 114,000 in 1891, and that of West Ham from 19,000 in 1851 to 267,000 in 1891. By the end of the century nearly 800,000 working men commuted daily from the suburbs to their places of employment in London.

So cheap transport and the huge city population made the demand for suburban housing of all complexions almost unending. There were also some charitable and philanthropic bodies building workers' housing during the nineteenth century, and those estates often carried much the same social stigma that some council estates can have today. But on the whole it was unfettered private enterprise which supplied both the middle and working classes with their houses – and very similar houses they were too. The biggest difference between the two types of housing was their size. The middle classes needed more space than the working classes, not for themselves but for the servants that were a concomitant of their position in society. In 1840 it was estimated that you needed a minimum salary of £150 a year to keep a servant; out of that salary you would pay £3 a year for a servant to come in and clean. At £200 per annum you could afford a resident maid at £9 a year, and if you could clear £250 a year you had arrived and your wife became a 'lady'.

It was more than snobbishness that made the developers aim for 'high-class' suburbs. Around 90 per cent of Victorians rented rather than purchased accommodation. This meant that if an area improved in status the landlords could swiftly raise rents to reflect this; it also meant that if an area dropped from favour the owners of its estates would find it hard to rent their investments at any price above the barest minimum. The house market was swift to react to the subtlest changes in the social standing of an area.

It was always, therefore, a developer's nightmare that somehow the seeds of a slum would take root in his district, blighting forever his chances of getting a return for his investment. The beginning of ruin was work. 'Essentially, slum areas were those in which the inhabitants lived cheek by jowl with the industrial enterprises in which they worked, which by their nature were often smelly or noisy or both,' wrote Gillian Tindall in her history of Kentish Town, *The Fields Beneath* (1977). 'It must have been partly a genuine objection to noise and smell which drove the middle classes to seek the new dormitory area further out, but it was also a matter of hardening lines of class demarcation.' For the investing landlord, and therefore also for the speculative builder and the developer, the most financially rewarding areas were those new middle-class dormitories. But building them and buying into them was a risky process.

The art was in reducing or offsetting that risk, and the person who carried most of the burden was the speculative builder. The spec builder really came into his own in London because of its curious lease system. The owner of a piece of land would parcel it up and lease it off to a builder, on the understanding that when the lease expired the houses the builder had erected would revert to the landowner. As an encouragement, the rent on the lease on each parcel of land would be very low for the first year or two, while the houses were being built. The landowner's risk was minimal – he received a rent for his land which perhaps represented a higher income than if he had grown crops on it, and at the end of the lease he would get back his land plus the property resting on it.

The spec builder, on the other hand, was risking quite a lot. He was usually a mason or bricklayer who had gone into business on his own account by borrowing money to buy a lease on enough land for two or three houses. He would build the houses as quickly as he could, and then sell them off to investors who would in turn rent them out. If anything went wrong it was the

Old weavers' houses at Bethnal Green in the East End of London.

builder who suffered: if bad weather, illness, a poor site or problems with the materials slowed him down, he would become more in debt to his creditors than he could afford; and if the houses that he built did not fetch the right price or took some time to sell, he was a broken man. Bankruptcy was all too common among builders of this nature. It is easy to see why these builders were conservative and why the houses they built tended to play safe. On the other hand the nineteenth-century builder was not burdened by the red tape that can so confine a modern builder. Only on the larger and more prestigious estates would the landowner lay down rules about the size and appearance of the houses to be built on his land; otherwise the builder was free to construct as he saw fit. It was not until relatively late in the century that any coherent local or national legislation was initiated to control the type and quality of his work.

Politicians nowadays are wont to look with envy at this apparent lack of bureaucracy and state interference during the nineteenth century. It is true that the industrial revolution needed no pump-priming from enterprise boards. But it is also true that there was little aid for those ground under the wheels of the revolution; the unemployed or sick survived as best they could on their own. Victorian society was not unlike a game of snakes and ladders: the few barriers of bureaucracy enabled your ascent to be meteoric, and the lack of safety nets meant that your descent could be even swifter. Builders were not the only people to suffer bankruptcy in a world where one slip in the cash flow could lead straight to the debtors' court. Dickens portrayed a world, not of heightened drama with artfully indulged tragedy, but of brutal reality. His work sold well partly because it revealed that world to the middle classes who had fled it.

Until the urbanization and suburbanization of society during the nineteenth century it was usual for master and servant to exist together, at each other's gate. The urban concentrations of squalor that became slums of unparalleled degradation, and the insecurities of the new-born middle classes, encouraged a separation between the two. Nobody who could afford to do otherwise wanted to live in close proximity to a rookery full of the desperate, the diseased, the starving and the criminal. The advantages of the suburbs were that they had yet to give root to slums, and that their very novelty freed them from such associations. The middle classes had the opportunity to make their world all over again – a nice, ordered, genteel, predictable world out of range of the malodorous slums at the centre of the cities. The slums, of course, could be visited by ladies intent on a little charitable work, but otherwise, as the century advanced, those slums became less bearable and less visible.

The rules and regulations of philanthropic housing estates, designed to house working-class people of good character, often contain strict instructions that the 'taking in' of work will mean instant eviction. And they meant it. The tenants' record books of these estates are full of curt remarks such as 'received notice' and 'notice to quit' for crimes like taking in a little laundry to help make ends meet. These estates were at the top end of the working-class housing market, and were built by organizations such as the Society for Improving the Condition of the Labouring Classes, established in 1844. Unlike other welfare societies and private philanthropists, however, it set itself the task of creating examples of good-quality working-class housing rather than supplying accommodation to a lower specification but in large quantity, such as London's Peabody estates and those initiated by Angela Burdett-Coutts. The philanthropic estates were too expensive for the majority of the poor to afford, and their stringent rules – designed to ensure not only cleanliness and godliness, but also Christian obedience – made them unpalatable to many more.

Peabody Square, Westminster, 1869: one of a series of philanthropic estates aimed at providing a decent standard of accommodation for working men and their families.

It was the mark of a slum-dweller to work from home. That work would cover anything from laundering clothes in the open sewers that still passed for rivers, to the dishonourable professions of bone-boiling, manure-making, soap manufacture, refuse-gathering and the training of fighting dogs. Like the slums themselves, proximity to work was avoided by those who could afford to. It was therefore a sign of wealth and respectability to live as far away from your work as possible. A Victorian gentleman merely asked that he be able to close the front door of his house on the noxious ambiance of the city when his work was done. The outside world could run its unfettered course, crushing whom it might, provided there was a haven of peace and security free from every element of that world – free from noise, dirt and commerce. The Victorians had invented the home.

Housework was equally tainted. The lady of the house, often a recent arrival to her station, concealed her ignorance of the practice of running a middle-class establishment and sought to distinguish herself from her servants, and ape the

A rare group portrait of the servants of a well-to-do household, *c.* 1880, each with the tools of his or her trade. From left to right: under-maid, coachman, housekeeper, gardener, cook, boot boy, nurse, under-gardener.

upper classes, by concentrating on managing them rather than the house. House management was the job of a housekeeper. The growth in the urban middle classes and the way in which they delegated many of the tasks previously managed by the mistress of the house created a big leap in demand for servants during the nineteenth century. As a result a whole new stratum of the population was introduced to the role of waiting on others. These new servants had neither the upbringing nor the background which would have educated them in the various arcane elements of their station, so they were forced to learn, often at short notice. If they could read, there were manuals on the arts of service. And matching the publications aimed at teaching servants their work were a complementary set teaching mistresses of households how to manage servants. While both sides were busily learning their new roles they were in fact collaborating in pushing out of the front and back doors of the house any task large enough to be labelled 'work'. Cleaning and cooking were only work for the servants. But as far as the titular heads of the house were concerned, the home was sacrosanct and inviolate from the mundane concerns of work and money.

Just as the demand for houses and the way they were run were undergoing a revolution, so were the methods – if not the styles – of construction of those houses. At the time of Cruikshank's early nineteenth-century print entitled *London Going Out of Town*, the first stage in developing any new fringe of the city was the erection of a brick kiln; in London this was easy, since the city lay on a convenient bed of clay. The bricks from the kiln would then supply the whole estate, which could sometimes be surprisingly small, since this was cheaper than trying to transport the bricks from elsewhere before the arrival of the railways and the cheap bricks they transported. A typical development might begin with a small farmer who was persuaded to lease off one or two fields for building and who then, perhaps with a little encouragement from the developers or builders, set himself up with a kiln to manufacture the bricks for the houses that soon started to cover his fields. Finally, to maintain a demand for his bricks he might lease out more of his land or he might even become a spec builder himself – from the country to the town in one generation. Around the middle of the century several things happened at once to affect the brick industry. Coal-firing of bricks was introduced, producing a more evenly 'cooked' product; and the brick press was brought into use, which ensured an evenness in size and consistency. The former variable brick was now being replaced by the standard brick. Then in 1850 the excise duty on bricks was abolished. And by now the spread of the railways meant that the bricks were universally available. It was no longer necessary to rely on local clay supplies. Bricks were cheap, and very much in demand.

The same was happening to glass. It had previously been a luxury material, not only because of the cost of manufacturing it but also because of the stringent excise duty and window tax, which effectively tripled the cost of an already expensive product. Excise duty was abolished in 1845, and window tax

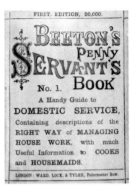

Mistress and servant alike learnt their skills from books and pamphlets like this.

Right: Crystal Palace, photographed by Delamotte in 1854 as it was being reconstructed at Sydenham after its removal from Hyde Park.

in 1851 – just in time for advantage to be taken of new manufacturing techniques in the construction of Joseph Paxton's Crystal Palace for the Great Exhibition. It was a glittering monument to glass and cast iron. Architectural historians are divided over whether the Crystal Palace was an innovation in building techniques, or whether it merely made use of techniques developed earlier. Whichever view is correct, the Crystal Palace was a prominent signpost for the future use of glass and triggered off the Victorians' long love affair with it.

The suburban spec builder now had a standard brick and a decent bit of glass; the railways also brought him Welsh or Westmorland slates and timber from wherever was cheapest. With his materials at the ready he could find a site and start work. The house he began to build was standard, too. Architects tended to be commissioned only for tasks somewhat larger or more sophisticated than the common or garden domestic house. Each builder would have had a dog-eared pattern book covering a variety of types of houses; there would be a picture of what it would look like when it was finished, a plan, and often a list of materials and specimen costs. It was a sort of Mrs Beeton for builders.

Coinciding with the standardization of materials and complementing the house styles common to pattern books of the period was a third element – legislation – which was beginning to ensure that houses were built to certain standards. For a long time there had been basic regulations concerning construction in the cities: as early as 1774 the party walls between terraces had to be thick enough to resist the spread of fire from one house to the next, and during the nineteenth century it was common to find local legislation insisting that builders adhere to the street's building line – in other words, the fronts of all buildings should not project beyond a certain point. From the 1840s onwards local legislation enforced more stringent controls over housing standards, and each city imposed certain guidelines about the type of housing that could be constructed and the facilities that should be incorporated in that house. The most far-reaching and effective of these was probably the Public Health Act of 1848, which made it obligatory for every household to have a fixed sanitary arrangement of some kind. This perhaps did less to improve the quality of sanitation than it did the style of house construction. Back-to-backs were frequently built around a small, dark court containing a single unsavoury privy shared by a number of households, and the local Act of 1844 in Manchester, for instance, requiring a privy or ash pit behind each house, effectively made back-to-back housing illegal in that city.

Then came another Public Health Act, in 1875, which gave local authorities the right to control house layouts, the width of new streets and the spaces around buildings, as well as sanitation and drainage. This was in turn followed by model by-laws from the Local Government Board, which were adopted by most local authorities though not necessarily all for the same reason. For the first time developers were obliged to give notice of their intentions, to deposit plans to allow their work to be inspected and, if it was not up to scratch, to pull it down again. Other by-laws were even more specific: houses had to have access to at least 150 square feet of open space, the windows of houses had to occupy at least 10 per cent of the ground area, and streets over 100 feet long had to be at least 36 feet wide and open at least at one end. This may sound odd to us today, but in the rookeries there was sometimes no appreciable way in and out of the slum and whole streets would be built over. Most cities adopted these measures in an effort to improve the health of their citizens. But London, a city built on leases, introduced its legislation – which was essentially similar in content and effect – in an effort to ensure that construction standards were maintained at a sufficient level to allow the buildings to last the length of their lease.

Lower middle-class aspirations satirized by George Du Maurier in *Punch*, 1871. The husband is shocked by his wife's request for a trip to the seaside now that they have the regulation tiny garden. Spec builders are still at work at the end of the terrace.

Whatever the rationale, the effect of the by-laws on housing was dramatic, partly because the legislation happened to coincide with the great building boom of the 1880s. Street after street of what came to be called 'by-law' housing went up, representing an enormous improvement in standards, especially for the working classes. There were airier streets; space at the backs of houses; better insulation against cold, damp and noise because of

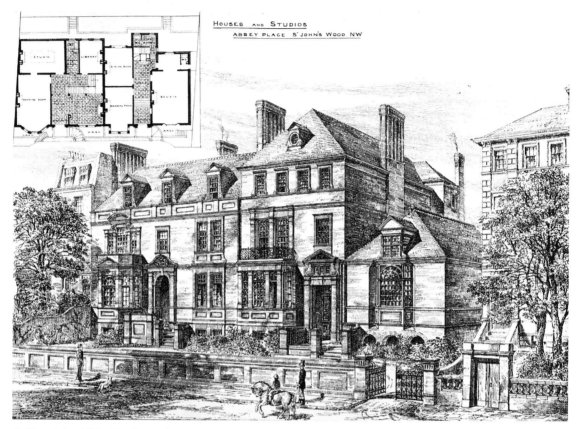

Architect-designed Abbey Place Studios, St John's Wood, London, depicted in *The Building News* of 18 January 1878, was a property at the top end of the social spectrum.

A typical new street of the 1870s, lined with modest terrace houses.

thicker walls; higher ceilings; larger windows; and wooden floors instead of flagstones. The Victorian builder was working with standardized materials from a set pattern of styles and plans, enjoined by legislation to meet a certain standard of workmanship and supplying a customer, of whatever class, who wanted a 'standard' house. So the spec builder built terrace after terrace after villa after villa of what we lump together today under the title 'Victorian houses'. Nobody had seen building on that scale before and it is unlikely that we will ever see it again. The Victorian house was a certain kind of domestic construction at its peak – a universal house for every Tom, Dick or Harry built by thousands of precariously industrious Toms, Dicks and Harrys.

2. How They Were Built

The Victorians invented jerry-building. The term, which first appeared in Liverpool in the 1830s, derived from 'jury-rig' and 'jury-mast' – naval terminology for temporary repairs. Jerry-building had in fact been going on long before the label was applied – the result of the rapid influx of immigrants to Liverpool and the consequent pressure on accommodation. To meet this demand the flimsiest of houses were thrown up, some with walls only half a brick thick – four and a half inches; many of them failed to survive the great storm of 1822. A grand jury referred to 'the slight and dangerous mode of erecting dwelling houses now practised in this town and neighbourhood'.

The Way We Build Now, an acid comment on contemporary building techniques from *Punch*.

When it became easier for builders to get credit, and the demand for housing moderated, the quality of workmanship improved. This is not to say that Victorian builders were perfect; as in any trade or profession, there were good and bad builders. This is reflected in the contradictory views expressed today: some say that Victorian houses are appalling examples of the builder's craft,

Right: Membership papers for the Operative Bricklayers' Society: an excellent example of late Victorian polychromatic brickwork.

A typical early Victorian terrace, in a currently fashionable area, as it looks today. Sadly, not all are as well-kept as this.

with thin walls, bowed roofs and no foundations to speak of; others that they represent the acme of achievement, a harmonious balance of materials, environment and purpose. It is true that most houses from the last century suffer from shallow foundations and understructured roofs, and that some of their construction methods are now illegal. But it is also true that the late Victorian house represents a century's worth of refinements in skills and materials. You can choose which side of the fence you want to sit on, provided you remember that the worst examples of Victorian housing have either fallen down or been demolished.

Good or bad, building in the nineteenth century was a skilled trade based on cheap, plentiful labour and a system of training established by the craft guilds to ensure that a 'man with a trade' was knowledgeable and experienced at his job.

A normal apprenticeship lasted five years, although it could be longer. At around the age of twelve or fourteen apprentices would become indentured to a craftsman, to be used – in the early years at least – as cheap assistants. Rates of pay were low, but apprenticeship was an investment for the future – having a trade was at least some guarantee of employment, and it also conferred a higher status than that of 'unskilled labourer'. The difference in pay alone was substantial. A skilled bricklayer could expect to be paid ten times as much as an unskilled hod-carrier, and the bricklayer – especially during the building booms – had work for most of the year. His occupation did not admit him to the middle classes but it allowed him, as a representative of the skilled working classes, to adopt many of the trappings of a middle-class lifestyle. Some idea of the status of a master craftsman is given by the fact that he was on a par with a jobbing architect at the beginning of the nineteenth century. With a modicum of success such a man might even end up living in one of the houses he had helped to build. Emboldened by this, his next step might be one that many nineteenth-century craftsmen took – to go into business on his own account and become a spec builder. If he survived the omnipresent risk of bankruptcy he might make a comfortable middle-class living. Some builders did even better. Thomas Cubitt, an imaginative builder responsible for many of the most fashionable parts of London during the last century, was even able to turn down a peerage.

More typical was the builder Edward Yates who, although he was the largest builder in South London during the 1880s, used methods common to most speculative builders of the period. A study carried out by Professor H.J. Dyos of the development of the South London suburb of Camberwell looked at Yates's methods in the construction of Dragon Road, on either side of which Yates ultimately built 46 two-storeyed terraced houses. He would acquire on a seventy-year lease a parcel of land sufficient for two or three houses, build on the land, and then buy a lease on the next parcel for the next few houses in the terrace. It was a laborious procedure made necessary by the way builders financed their business. Yates's capital was raised by mortgages from building societies and solicitors, probably at the rate of 5 per cent interest over fourteen years. A completed house cost about £190 to build and could be let at an annual rent of about £26. His houses survived until the 1950s, when they were demolished to make way for what is now Burgess Park.

Yates chose to let the houses himself. Most spec builders, however, lived a hand-to-mouth existence and could not afford to let the houses they had built. It was more usual for them to raise a mortgage on a floor of the house they were building in order to finance the next stage; then when the house was built they would sell it off at a price to cover the costs of labour, materials and mortgage and allow a small margin for profit. Some builders were so small that they might only build one house a year, occupying the rest of their time with repair work to keep their labour force together. Builders this small found it hard to get the sort of financing that Yates used, and often relied on the landlord himself to supply credit either in the form of money or even sometimes in bricks. These small fish formed very complex financial and working relationships in order to survive.

Big or small, each fish sooner or later was confronted with a plot of land that was to be his building site. He would dig a hole. If the house was to have a cellar the hole would be a big one, but if the house was to be cellarless the hole might be extremely shallow. A lot of modern owners of Victorian houses complain of damp in their cellars. The original owners noticed this problem too: in her book *From Kitchen to Garret* (1888) Mrs Panton says tartly that cellars

The kind of farm that hungry cities were to turn into building sites. This one once stood in Earls Court, now a traffic-filled, densely populated part of west London.

are 'simply used as a deposit for all the surface water which accumulates mysteriously around the ordinary "jerry-built" mansion of the suburban builder'. She was speaking of the London suburbs, which frequently suffered from the high watertable caused by the raft of clay on which London is sited. The water problem varied from site to site. Current owners of damp basements have little to worry about unless the cellar is actually under water, although they may be concerned by the variety of fungi encouraged by these damp conditions. The lime in the mortar and in the annual distemper wash that the Victorians would apply to their cellars had a mild fungicidal effect. Modern owners who have attempted to cure the problems of water and fungi by completely waterproofing their cellars at great expense have sometimes found that they have merely moved the problem to another part of the house. This is the first hint that the Victorian house is a cohesive entity that needs careful consideration before alteration.

On the other hand, many an old house is standing despite apparently terminal mistreatment. With space at a premium, cellars are a popular 'original feature' with today's buyers and estate agents alike – it is one of the things that distinguishes an old house from a modern Wimpey or Barratt estate. But not every old house has a cellar, so more adventurous owners of houses from the last century are digging underneath their floorboards to *make* a cellar. Provided the walls of the basement give plenty of leeway to the foundations a surprising amount of storage or utility space can be gained without any apparent damage to the structure of the house. The success of this operation depends on judging the site and the house carefully before starting work; there could have been a reason why the original builder avoided installing a cellar.

The foundations of a house, as every Victorian knew from his Bible, should be based on something solid, but circumstances often militated against this in practice. Sometimes there was too little money for the builder to waste time digging deep enough, and sometimes the site offered little but the watertable as a solid basis. Whatever the reasons, the Victorian house is reputed to suffer from one very common defect – inadequate or no foundations. But before you start worrying about your Victorian house take a look around you – there are a remarkable number of houses from that period which are still standing upright after a century or so, despite these shallow foundations.

Assuming that the spec builder had the time and inclination to do the job properly, he would begin by digging a trench six or seven bricks deep. He would then lay a footing six bricks wide for his base, which would narrow with each successive layer of bricks until it was up to ground level and the required width for the wall of the house. Under ideal conditions this would give the house ample roots, but there was such pressure on land for building during the nineteenth century that sites were often less than ideal. The Hackney Marshes in London barely escaped being built over, and the equally swampy Stoke Newington first became a spoil heap for the refuse from railway construction before succumbing to the suburb fever generated by those railways. The ground in Stoke Newington is so spongy that underpinning of foundations is almost commonplace today. This is done by digging down and infilling with concrete under a section of the original foundations; when that concrete is set the next section is attended to, and so on until the whole house is underpinned. A modern builder engaged in this painstaking pursuit on a house in Stoke Newington protested when the District Surveyor stipulated that the new foundations had to go down 6 feet. 'You're lucky,' retorted the District Surveyor, 'I made the people along the road dig down 20 feet.'

A lot of London houses have similar problems. Being built on the raft of clay has cushioned them against many of the shocks, from Second World War bombs to modern-day juggernauts, that should have damaged such insecurely founded buildings. But movement in that clay can sometimes be even more damaging: in the long hot summer of 1976, for instance, the clay substratum began to dry out and shrink, leaving many shallow foundations unsupported. The opposite can also happen. If saturated clay soil freezes it will expand, pushing the shallow foundations upwards. On any typical cold winter's day paving stones are pushed up all over London because of the frost. In southern England frost is assumed to reach no further than 18 inches below ground, however, so if your foundations are deeper than that you should be safe – if you live in southern England.

Wet sites were not unfamiliar to the Victorian spec builder, then, and to cope with them he might have to abandon brick foundations altogether. One house in South London suffering from subsidence after the drought of 1976 had to have its foundations excavated in order to repair the damage. The modern builder was astonished to find that the house was built on foundations not of brick, but of broken up ceramic lemonade bottles. In such conditions it was more common to use timber pile foundations driven into the waterlogged ground to form the basis for the house. Strangely enough, so long as the ground remains waterlogged these timbers will not decay. But a drop in the watertable allows decay to start to set in and subsidence may follow. However the Victorian house did have, and still has, ways of coping with such movement.

In a way, Victorian cities solved the problem of wet building sites and damp basements by their thirst for water – a vital component in industrial processes ranging from engineering to brewing. Since about 1850 the watertable under

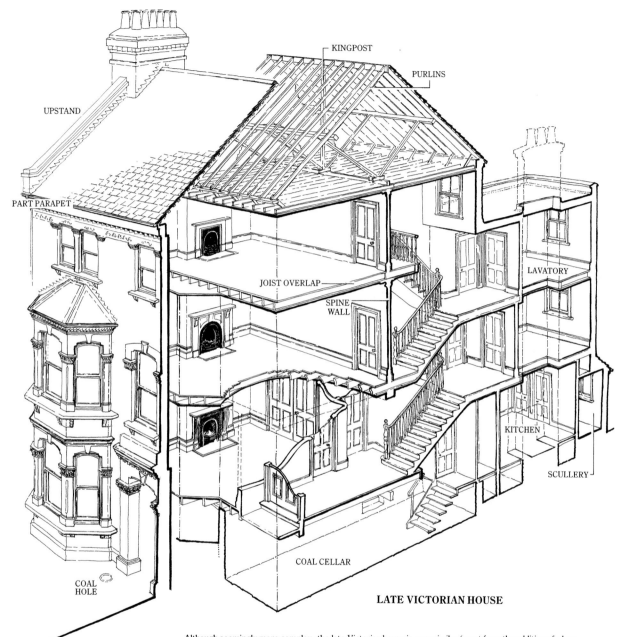

KINGPOST

PURLINS

UPSTAND

PART PARAPET

JOIST OVERLAP

SPINE
WALL

LAVATORY

KITCHEN

SCULLERY

COAL CELLAR

COAL
HOLE

LATE VICTORIAN HOUSE

Although seemingly more complex, the late Victorian house is very similar (apart from the addition of a bay window, a back extension and some decorative stucco) to its Georgian-style counterpart (p. 51). There is still a part parapet half concealing the pitched roof. Off-the-peg plaster mouldings and sash windows have been used. The kitchen, scullery and accompanying bells are now in a back extension. This house probably only had day servants, so there was no need for servants' sleeping quarters (although sometimes maids were expected to sleep under the kitchen table). As an advance on the Georgian-style house there is now a coal hole at the front door to prevent dirt being tramped through the hall every time fuel was delivered. There may even have been a lavatory built into the house in one of the rooms of the back extension, which would be roofed in either asphalt or rolled lead. The walls get thinner storey by storey, the fireplaces, mouldings and skirting boards become plainer, and the joists overlap on the spine wall.

cities like London, Birmingham and Liverpool has dropped steadily, until by 1950 the water under some of these cities was anything from 900 to 1200 feet below its original level. But since 1950, because of falling industrial demand reinforced by economic recession, the watertable has started to rise again. In an article in *New Scientist* (27 March 1986) Ted Nield takes as an example the district of Witton in Birmingham:

In the 1950s there were just 30 firms in Witton. By 1968 there were 22, and by 1984 just 12. Among the closures were two large consumers of water, Ansell's brewery and the gas works. But the area has also lost a food-processing firm, a heavy engineering company and a power station. These closures have meant a huge fall in demand for water, from 20 million litres/day in the 1950s to 2 or 3 million litres/day, in a little over 30 years. The water table in Witton has risen by as much as 5 metres since 1972.

Although water has started spilling into underground tunnels it is unlikely to have much effect on the foundations of Victorian houses – at least in the short term – especially those built on clay soil, which should form an impervious barrier to the climbing water. The real danger is from sewer contamination. The durability of the Victorian house and the progressive fragility of century-old sewers have the same roots – mortar.

The Victorian builder used a lime-based mortar which he would make up on-site. There were many regional variations, but they all shared certain characteristics that are vital to the continued existence of Victorian houses.

The Vaughan Library in Harrow, showing the extent to which decoration, including polychromatic bricks and tiles, could be applied to Victorian buildings.

These mortars are weak, flexible and porous, which means that they give an old house considerable freedom to bulge and sag before any cracks start appearing in the walls. When the movement gets more extreme it is the mortar that fails before anything else, leaving the bricks undamaged and easily repaired with a little repointing. The porosity of the mortar may seem a problem these days when we battle to keep creeping damp at bay. It is, however, an advantage in Victorian houses with solid walls, because it allows those walls to breathe, letting water evaporate outwards rather than trapping it within the masonry to cause problems. Because modern cement-based mortars are impervious to water they will actually trap it within the walls of the house, causing rather than solving the problem of damp.

Having built his foundation, all the builder had to do was to lay one brick on top of another, with a little mortar between, until he had a house. It sounds simple, but it is just the beginning of the arcane complexities that give a building its personality. Depending on the period of building and whereabouts in Britain he was working, the brick the builder was using could have been anything from London stock – a distinctive yellow brick – to Staffordshire blues – coloured by the high iron content in the clay and more often used for bridges. There was a huge variety of bricks available to the Victorian builder and he knew how to use them. The polychromatic and decorative brickwork of the Gothic Revival of the 1850s and 1860s, that has become one of the hallmarks of the Victorian age, depended to no small extent on the subtle deployment of bricks called red builders. These were red, sand-faced bricks soft enough to be rubbed into the shape desired; hence their other name, rubbers. Rubbers are the bricks used to give the rounded edges to decorative arches and lintels.

There were almost as many ways of laying the bricks as there were kinds of bricks; the commonest style of the Victorian period was Flemish bond, in which stretchers (bricks laid lengthwise) were punctuated by headers (bricks laid crosswise so that they only showed their head in the finished wall). This produced a strongly bonded solid wall. Today's building regulations insist on a cold-, damp- and noise-reducing cavity wall for houses – a wall that is in fact two walls with a gap between. As a result Flemish bond has been abandoned for stretcher bond – all the bricks are laid lengthwise. The problems occur when you want to match the old with the new; if, for example, you want to build a modern extension on to a Victorian house. Aesthetically minded owners may prefer a bond that matches the original bond of the house, but the extension has to have its cavity wall to conform with the regulations. The compromise is to fake the appearance of Flemish bond by using what are called snapped headers or half bats – bricks that have been cut in half to provide the header part of the bond without jutting into the cavity between the walls. It costs a little more, but many people think it is worth it.

Before you contemplate such an undertaking, however, look carefully at your house. One of the bugbears of matching new bricks to old is their variability not only in colour and quality but also in size. You may find that new bricks are too big, too, and for precisely these reasons there is now a thriving market in secondhand bricks. By dint of a little digging around in architectural salvage yards you may be lucky enough to find, at an affordable price, the original size and colour of brick to match your house. Remember that until the mid-nineteenth century brick-manufacturing was a very local industry, so if your house is of this period you are most likely to find the right sort of bricks close to home.

As the brick walls climbed higher, so other problems arose for the Victorian builder. The house was usually a minimum of two storeys tall, which meant that the wall would have to support two floors and a roof as well as itself. The higher the wall the less it had to support, so it could be made thinner to reduce the amount of bricks needed and to lessen the weight on the wall and its foundations beneath. This reduction was done floor by floor: at the beginning of each floor the wall would reduce by half a brick thickness, and the shelf created was used to support the floor joists. Alternatively, if the builder was trimming his costs by keeping his walls thin all the way up – not uncommon – the joist would lie on a cross-timber inserted while the wall was being built. Even these could be dispensed with *in extremis* by leaving out a few bricks at the appropriate point in the wall to form a pocket in which to place the joists. This kind of exposed timber makes dry rot a common problem in Victorian houses.

It was this desire to use as few bricks as possible that partly accounts for the widespread popularity of the terraced house among builders of the period. It was also a very sound structural form that could withstand a fair amount of skimped workmanship before anything disastrous resulted. The terrace was constructed on the domino principle – each wall supported by its neighbour. This was fine in the middle of a terrace, but a little more problematic at the end of the row, where the walls have to resist a tendency to collapse under their own weight. In most terraces this tendency is not helped by the position of the stairwell against the outside wall of the end house. There is very little holding that wall up, or on to the house. This is why tie bars or signs of rebuilding can often be seen on the end walls of terraces. The front and back walls are tied together by the floor and ceiling joists that run front-to-back (although in some houses joists can run from side to side, leaving front and back walls untied), resting on a central structural partition.

A Georgian-style terrace secured by tie bars through the end wall (left).

When you were building a terrace you not only saved bricks by having two of your four walls common, but you could also save in labour costs. (Back-to-backs, which continued to be built in some parts of the country into the early twentieth century, saved even more bricks.) Those party walls that allowed you to save on bricks would ultimately be the internal walls of the houses and would be covered with plaster. Since the brickwork would be unseen, you could use apprentice bricklayers and cheap brick – often mis-shaped reds – to construct those walls; the visible back and front walls of a house required qualified craftsmen. When the external walls reached the party walls there were often disagreements over how the walls should meet, and it is not uncommon to find that the external walls of a terrace bond only grudgingly with the party walls.

As well as keeping the neighbours apart and acting as a firebreak, the party walls worked in tandem with the spine wall – usually a wall running from one party wall to the other through the centre of the house – in keeping the roof up and the front and back walls together. When builders had difficulty finding joist timbers long enough to run front-to-back they would overlap shorter timbers at the spine wall. That wall is usually the one that separates the front and back rooms of a house, and therefore the wall that most people want to knock through when they decide to open up their house. This is not a decision to take lightly. A badly calculated removal of part of the spine wall can transfer unevenly through the remainder of the wall the strain of holding up the roof or holding in the exterior walls. As a result the foundations will be depressed, causing subsidence and even deflection further up the structure. Deflection is a polite way of saying that the exterior walls have started to peel away from the main structure or to collapse under their own weight. There are, however, other reasons for cracks appearing in exterior walls, and their appearance does not necessarily mean that a wall is deflecting.

Irish immigrants flooding into England since the late 1840s established a stereotype that lingers today. The immigrants not only supplied the cheap labour for jerry-built houses but also had to live in them.

The internal walls of the house were often made from timber-framed partitions called stud walls, which were covered by lath and plaster. You can easily tell the difference by rapping on the wall with your knuckles: a solid wall will hurt your knuckles; a plaster wall has more give to it (easier on the knuckles) and makes a hollow sound. Just to confuse you, stud walls were sometimes filled in with brick rather than lath. If you plan a total redecoration of your house involving stripping off old wallpaper down to the plaster, check a small sample before you start. Sometimes the plaster in old houses has lost its key and the only thing keeping that plaster on the wall is the wallpaper.

A no doubt apocryphal story is told of a young couple spurred into action by a colour supplement article on how to knock through non-load-bearing walls. They followed to the letter the diagram provided and, covered with plaster dust, retired to the pub for refreshment. Unfortunately, due to a proof-reading error the arrows indicating load- and non-load-bearing walls had been transposed. The hapless couple returned at closing time to find the best part of their abode in the cellar. The moral of this tale is that you should never rush into this kind of undertaking without scrupulous checking, and that it is safer to assume that all the walls in your Victorian house are load-bearing until proved otherwise. Even those fragile lath and plaster stud walls often support a prop holding up a vital bit of the roof – a makeshift queenpost, for those who like their terminology exact. Such measures are not uncommon in Victorian houses, because they almost always suffer from an understructured roof.

The architect Charles Eastlake, writing in the late nineteenth century, stated – typically for his period – that he disliked the style of Georgian housing that had preceded his own era. He was, however, forced to concede that the quality of workmanship was higher in Georgian buildings, because it was harder to conceal bad work. He blames this change on the advent of stucco:

What the general public does not know is that the structural deceits which it conceals are daily becoming so numerous and flagrant that they positively endanger life and property.

The results were there for all to see:

A few years have made [the house] a dingy abode: a few more years will make it a ghastly ruin. . . . An Englishman's house was formerly said to be his castle, but in the hands of the speculative builder and advertising tradesman, we may be grateful that it does not oftener become his tomb.

The term 'stucco' was first used by Italian craftsmen to define a grade of plaster, but it soon became a generic term for any kind of external plasterwork. It appealed strongly to Georgian and, in turn, Victorian builders and architects (apart from Mr Eastlake) as a way of dignifying otherwise mean and nasty structures, usually by moulding it into an imitation of stonework. It did have the supposed merit of waterproofing thin brick walls or ones made of soft, porous brick, and thus saving on construction costs. It could resist wind-blown rain that brickwork would otherwise absorb, but any rainwater accumulating on the

stucco was drawn by capillary action into the brickwork. However the amount of water involved was usually slight, and the Victorian house is as good at exhaling moisture as it is at absorbing it. Stucco could conceal a multitude of sins, but it also had practical and aesthetic purposes that suited it to Victorian houses.

There is an architectural truism that says that all a house needs is a good hat and a good pair of boots – meaning that a dry roof and solid foundations are the pre-requisites of a well-built house. The roof of a Victorian house does more than keep the rain out; it keeps the house up. It was the final element that balanced the various forces running through the house into a harmonious and durable construction. The foundations hold up and hold together the walls, which hold up and are tied together (hopefully) by the floor joist and the tie beam or ceiling joists, which in turn close the triangle formed by the rafters of the roof. The house may seem a complex structure; stripped down to its basic form, however, it is not only simple but also satisfyingly economical and self-sufficient.

Roofs are intimidating things: anything you encounter 30 feet or more up a bouncing ladder is bound to impress. However, the elements that make up a roof, like the elements that make up the whole house, are simple and logical. The majority of Victorian roofs were clad with slates or tiles hung on timber battens which ran across the rafters of the roof. Just as the amount of foundation and brickwork needed to keep the house up was nicely judged to its minimum, so the timbers used in the roof were used as sparingly as possible, with the result that most Victorian roofs are today considered understructured. If left to their own devices for a century or so they can begin to look distinctly bowed down by the weight of their slates. When a householder today decides to replace the slates on an old house with modern concrete tiles, he or she may be committing more than an aesthetic solecism, for the extra weight of the concrete tiles may exceed the abilities of the old roof timbers to support it. If the roof is not already bowed it soon will be, and some roof supports have collapsed under the strain. And because the Victorian house is such a nicely balanced structure, once the roof collapses a great deal of strain is thrown on to the walls, which may or may not be able to cope with it. In other words, any shift or change in the structure of a Victorian house affects the whole. By neglecting one area of your house you could be storing up problems in several places at once. If you need a new roof, a reputable builder ought to strengthen the roof timbers before laying concrete tiles.

The commonest form of roof in Victorian houses is the pitched or ridge roof; the name is self-explanatory once you have seen one. It is also called the couple

The façade of Linley Sambourne House, now preserved by the Victorian Society. Note the ebullient use of decorative stucco, the Wardian cases on the windowsills of the ground- and first-floor windows, and the grilles above the bay windows covering the under-floor ventilators for the gas lights.

close roof, because the rafters that lean against each other are coupled at the bottom by a collar beam or a ceiling joist, completing a triangle of timbers and forming a strong, coherent unit. This basic triangle could be elaborated by the addition of subsidiary supports – a central vertical timber called a kingpost or a matched pair of vertical timbers connected by a 'straining' beam called queenposts. Quite sophisticated carpentry would have been required to join these timbers to each other were it not for the use of a wide variety of ironmongery that made life easier for the nineteenth-century builder. To the inexperienced modern eye a loft can look unnecessarily cluttered by subsidiary timbers festooned with rusting lumps of iron. Cast or wrought iron fittings are not really harmed by a patina of rust, and the timbers they connect are vital to the integrity of your roof. Leave them both alone.

A fine example of the nineteenth-century love of decorative ironwork, with High Victorian cresting and finials on the roofline and balconies.

The rather basic nature of a pitched roof means that it is very good at what it does – keeping the house dry and all in one piece. Another common form of roof, which was developed during the Georgian period, has problems with both those functions. It is called the valley gutter or butterfly roof, and it could be seen as an inversion of the pitched roof. Instead of reaching up to a point so that rainwater runs down the roof to gutters at the edge of the house, it funnels that rain into a gutter running down the centre of the roof. Again the name is obvious once you have seen the roof. What may seem at first wilfully bad

Right: Stafford Terrace, London: a typical white-painted stucco frontage with black railings.

engineering does confer some architectural advantages: it allows a flat front to the house or terrace, the roof itself being concealed behind a parapet; and because the central valley gutter takes the rainwater off the roof and carries it to the back of the houses there is no need for unsightly guttering and drainpipes at the front of the house.

The provision and positioning of drainpipes is something that most people ignore until they see how unsightly a badly positioned downpipe can be. It is a problem that architects at all periods have devoted some time to solving. If you look carefully at certain houses you will realize that the elegant pillarwork running up the façade is actually doing the job of concealing a downpipe. At Linley Sambourne House in London, run by the Victorian Society, an even more sophisticated ploy was adopted. The front gutters of the terrace are piped through the space between the attic floor and the ceiling of the third floor to the back of the house, where it joins a conventional downpipe, so that the façade is not cluttered with piping. Over the years this pipe has sagged in the middle, however, so that there is always a pool of water in the centre of the house; it shows itself in bad weather by seeping through the ceiling under the inexorable urge of gravity.

A similar problem is experienced with valley gutter roofs. The central guttering can often become blocked with leaves and debris, causing water to build up until it seeps under the slates and into the roof space. Worse still, the beam that supports the gutter may sag with age – especially if it is undersized, as Victorian roof timbers often are. This causes water to pool in the middle of the roof and often cracks the guttering and allows that water to seep into the timbers, which sooner or later will start to rot and ultimately to collapse.

The other major disadvantage of a valley gutter roof is that it rarely provides a usable amount of loft or attic space. If all you require is room for a couple of trunks, a cold water cistern and an expansion tank for the central heating, this should not worry you. On the other hand, these drawbacks may become a virtue if you do want to convert your loft, however little space it offers. Because the roof is hidden from sight behind a parapet you can get away with things that would be difficult or impossible to do with a conventional pitched roof. Planning authorities and neighbours often object to you placing a dormer window in the roof on the side facing the road. (This not only ruins the line of the terrace but can, if done incorrectly, cause problems with the roof at a later date.) Those problems still exist if you put a dormer window or two in your valley gutter roof, but at least neither the planning authorities nor the neighbours can see the window and therefore will leave you in peace and not make objections to your planning application.

This early Victorian house is almost wholly Georgian in style – flat-fronted, arched windows, fanlight above the front door, and a parapet concealing the valley gutter roof. The upstand separating the roof of this house from the next one in the terrace was designed to act as a firebreak. The kitchen and servants' quarters would have been in the basement, although in some houses of the period the kitchen was placed in a back extension to keep smells and fire risks at arm's length. The valley gutter feeds all the rainwater to the back of the house, and even these relatively shallow foundations 'step up' to become walls. The walls themselves get thinner storey by storey. The brickwork of the walls concealed the true extent of the sash windows. The windows on the stairwell are designed to make the best use of natural light.

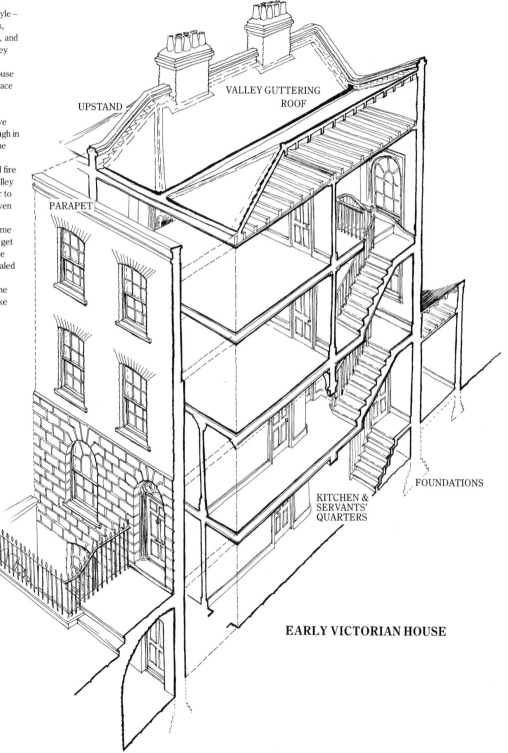

UPSTAND

VALLEY GUTTERING
ROOF

PARAPET

FOUNDATIONS

KITCHEN &
SERVANTS'
QUARTERS

EARLY VICTORIAN HOUSE

The window is an important architectural and structural element of the Victorian house. The kind most commonly found are sash windows – a peculiarity of British and Dutch architecture, much rarer elsewhere in Europe. Technically these windows are referred to as double-hung sash windows. They have vertically sliding sashes hung on flax cords or chains that are attached to counterweights concealed in boxes at either side of the window frame. Often the true size of these sash boxes is hidden by embedding them into the brickwork surrounding the window. The sash window is a complex piece of machinery, usually mass-produced for Victorian houses, but even so the modern householder may have difficulty buying replacements off the peg. Like bricks, windows vary subtly in size and design. A look at the Brooking Collection (p.170) of windows, which demonstrates the variety not just in size but also in profiling of the timber glazing bars, should give an inkling of the problem.

There seems little point in systematically and expensively eliminating all the features that distinguish a Victorian terrace.

Given the relative complexity and variety of the sash window, remarkably little has been done to aid the householder in its maintenance. The commonest problem is the sash cord itself: it breaks. Replacement of the cord is theoretically simple – you can find sash cord at most ironmongers. The difficulties begin when to try to install this new cord. To get into the sash box to attach the new cord to the weight you must first remove both sliding sections of the window. In theory this is accomplished by prising away the beading on one side of the window frame. The beading is supposed to be lightly pinned in and should lift away easily with the aid of a chisel. In practice is will have been painted so many times since it was last taken off that it will be almost impossible to remove without a modicum of violence and bad language. However, by causing a certain amount of damage to the paintwork you will eventually get the beading away from the window and be able to heave the heavy frame holding the glass on to the living room carpet. A pity you forgot to put down some newspaper. The rest is simple: before you move the window unpin the other cord (you may as well replace them both while you are at it), knotting it to stop it disappearing into the sash box. With the window now out of the way, the panel that gives access to the weight is exposed. Remove the panel, untie the old cord, tie the new cord *and* the old one to the weight and then draw the old one out, thus pulling the new cord through. Check the length, nail it to the window, place the window back in position, replace the beading and repaint the window frame. While you have the window out you may as well wash it – there is always a bit of sash window you cannot reach when you are trying to clean a third-floor window from the inside. But there is an easier way. . . .

With a certain amount of chauvinistic pride the authors would like to point out a Scottish variant of the sash window that copes with both of these difficulties. The windows are constructed in exactly the same manner as their southern equivalent with the exception of the beading on one or both sides of the frame. This is not nailed in, but attached by means of screws with knurled heads. It is therefore easy to unscrew and remove the beading, often without damage even to the paintwork. To aid the removal of the windowpane a pair of hinges is supplied for both frames. Just hook the window on to its hinges and open it out – sash box maintenance and window cleaning made easy. Even Charles Brooking of the Brooking Collection is not sure why this tiny innovation has never caught on south of the border.

The waywardness of sash windows, combined with the difficulty of making them draughtproof or combining them with secondary double glazing, has encouraged many householders to replace them with modern casement windows. Casement windows in themselves are no new thing. Examples of casements can be found in European architecture going back for centuries. The sash window developed during the Queen Anne period, was refined by the Georgians, and became central to the appearance of Victorian architecture. One of the reasons for its popularity was that it allowed a room to be ventilated more effectively than did a casement. The open bottom half of the sash allowed cool, fresh air to enter, and the open top half allowed the hot, used-up air –

which would naturally rise – to escape. Unfortunately this cycle of air is sometimes effected even when the window is closed. But the Victorians decided that sash windows were more suited to their post-post-post-Renaissance style of architecture. This is why the installation of modern casements can rouse shrieks of dismay from the neighbours as they see the visual continuity of their terrace being ruined by the intrusion of metal-framed windows designed to cope with a helicopter landing on the front lawn. Might the money have been better spent on restoring the original sash windows so that they were watertight and draughtproof? Victorians had the choice between casements and sash windows, and they chose sashes.

The most complex type of window you are likely to encounter in an ordinary Victorian house is the bay window. There were several reasons for its popularity, which goes back to the mid-eighteenth century. As an external architectural feature it broke up the sheer elevation of a row of terrace fronts, giving them a feeling of depth and texture. The projecting bay would catch sunlight that a flat window would merely observe. The main reason for its use

Part of a terrace with bay windows, designed to catch the sunshine and the eye of the prospective householder. The tiled porch and other decorative detailing are typical of late Victorian house design.

was simpler, however. It looked expensive. With a bit of embellishment, and a little detailing on the porch, the frontage of a house could be made to look a great deal more lovingly and carefully constructed than it in fact was. Therefore even the cheapest dwellings were often blessed with a bay window.

The final part of the construction of a Victorian house would be the stairs. These were usually wooden, and even the cheapest staircase required a surprising amount of joinery. The staircase tends to be one of the largest assemblies of timber in a typical house, and is particularly susceptible to attack from dry rot or insects. Most under-stair spaces are poorly ventilated, warm and damp – ideal conditions for dry rot. The skeins of fungus may be very extensive before they are noticed. Often they may not be apparent until the plastered soffit – the exposed side of the treads – is ripped away to reveal the state of the laths. Some architects and surveyors claim to be able to find dry rot by sense of smell. It smells, they say, not unlike human urine.

If a staircase is infected with dry rot the entire timber construction will have to be removed and replaced; if the stair is a simple one it may well be worth adapting a standard prefabricated type sold through DIY outlets. The major difference between a modern staircase of this type and the old one will be one of pitch, especially in small houses where the original staircase is likely to be pitched at what is now an illegally steep angle, using high risers and narrow treads. Insect infestation, if caught early enough, is a lot less serious. The timber will need treating with an insecticide and checking to see whether any of the structure needs replacement, but otherwise the stairs will be safe.

The handrail and balusters – the uprights that run from the handrail to the tread of the staircase – of Victorian stairs come in a range of styles and profiles. For the purist this can be an area of specialization in itself. For the householder bent on restoring his house – especially if the staircase has been damaged by being boxed in – replacement wooden balusters to match the originals can often be easily obtained through specialist dealers such as architectural salvage or period joinery firms. The fashion for boxing in staircases because they were dust-traps now appears to have lapsed; modern vacuum cleaners deal with the dirt quickly and efficiently. Boxing in not only destroyed the aesthetic balance of the stairs, but on a much more practical level made them unnecessarily dark and oppressive. Spec builders did not spend a penny more than was absolutely necessary to sell their houses, yet even the meanest and least decorated house would have had what is to our eyes a decorative staircase. To the builder, used to putting up houses that made the best use of natural light since artificial light was so poor, that style of staircase was purely functional. The handrail supported you, and the balusters let the light through to help you see your

way. It was yet another example of the functionalism that underlies the individual elements of a Victorian house.

That functionalism is often obscured by time. We live our lives in a very different way from the Victorians, and we see our world differently too. It is commonplace to describe a terrace as a collection of uniform houses which rely on their unanimity and anonymity for architectural integrity. But they are more than a repetition of a single form; they are also, collectively, one building, often with decorative detailing at either end and a portico-like cornice in the centre to emphasize that entity. To alter one house in a terrace is not unlike changing a small part of the frontage of one house: it looks odd and asymmetrical.

The Victorian house evolved much more slowly than any modern equivalent. The methods and materials used in its construction had the time to become refined: a late Victorian house was based on technology that had been tested for over a century. Victorian houses, especially in London, fetch high prices; it is worth thinking carefully before you modernize your Victorian house into extinction.

A terrace is an architectural whole and looks best when treated as such.

3. The Home Within

Most Victorians rented their houses and therefore had little control over their external appearance. Charles Eastlake caustically observed that 'the practice of training ivy and creepers from the basement storey to the first floor, and that of filling the drawing room balcony with flowering plants . . . is really the best means by which we can invest our street fronts, as they are at present designed, with even the smallest degree of interest'. Instead, income and interest were concentrated on the interior of the house.

Rent alone could absorb a large proportion of the disposable income of a middle-class Victorian. In *New Grub Street* (1891) George Gissing describes the life of a respectable widow of restricted circumstances:

Like the majority of London people, she occupied a house of which the rent absurdly exceeded the due proportion of her income, a pleasant foible turned to such good account by London landlords. Whereas she might have lived with a good deal of modest comfort, her existence was a perpetual effort to conceal the squalid background of what was meant for the eyes of her friends and neighbours. She kept only two servants, who were so ill paid and so relentlessly overworked that it was seldom that they remained with her for more than three months.

She was afraid of sliding down the social scale into the world of Mr Pooter. 'The Laurels', Brickfield Terrace, Holloway – a nice six-roomed residence with one servant – was the epitome of lower middle-class life. George and Weedon Grossmith's *The Diary of a Nobody* (1892) begins with an idyllic description of the everyday existence of Mr Pooter and his darling wife Caroline:

There is always something to be done: a tin tack here, a Venetian blind to put straight, a fan to nail up, or a carpet to nail down – all of which I can do with my pipe in my mouth; while Carrie is not above putting a button on a shirt, mending a pillowcase, or practising the 'Sylvia Gavotte' on our new cottage piano (on the three years' system), manufactured by V. Bilkson (in small letters), from Collard and Collard (in very large letters).

The respectable widow and the Pooters both expended an enormous amount of energy and income on their houses in a way that would seem excessive to us now. According to Mrs Panton, the prospective lessee of a house should allow about 10 per cent of his income for rent and taxes. Of the rest some went to pay for servants, food, fuel and clothing, but a remarkable amount was expended on furnishing the house. The nearest modern equivalent is perhaps the money people spend on buying and maintaining a car.

The care lavished on the furnishing of a typical middle-class Victorian household was part and parcel of the development of the idea that the house was a haven from the nasty and complicated business of work. Until the nineteenth century there had been surprisingly few boundaries between the public and private areas of a house. During the eighteenth century it was claimed that a true gentleman should live as though his entire life were public. If this seems egotistical, remember that an eighteenth-century gentleman was surrounded by servants and the only sensible way to behave was as if a servant was always present or about to be present. The ubiquity of servants could lead to them appearing at the most inopportune moments.

The Victorian era was characterized not by this kind of aristocratic panache but rather by a middle-class doggedness. This newly numerous and powerful stratum of society wanted rules to live by and to enable them to know the right thing to do at the right moment. So they created those guidelines, and tried to limit the occasions when they would be expected to do the right thing. They were rather like actors, carefully learning their parts by rote from books and magazines, going out on to the stage to play those parts as best they knew how, and returning to the wings exhausted and desperate, finding there a refuge which would allow them to drop the subterfuge. The outside of a Victorian house was a mask to conceal the actors within.

The occupants divided the house into three main areas: the public, the private and the unmentionable. The public areas were much as one would expect: the hall, drawing room, morning room perhaps, dining room and – if a man visited – perhaps also the study. The remainder of the house was not as private and inviolate as it may at first seem. Servants were specifically instructed not to knock on the doors of rooms before entering except in the case of bedrooms, dressing rooms and, in the latter part of the century, bathrooms. This can partly be explained by the status of servants, which was so low that they were not considered worthy of constant acknowledgement by the family. More practically, if servants begged entrance every time they had work to do in a room there would be little time left for them to complete their assigned tasks, which were all too numerous as it was.

So the only truly private rooms for the Victorian family would be their bedrooms and dressing rooms. Home manuals of the time advised hanging curtains in front of bedroom doors in case the inhabitant should inadvertently leave the door open at an unfortunate moment. Servants did, of course, have access to these rooms to clean them, to supply water for washing and, in the case of grander households, to help the lady of the house with her toilet and dress.

Woman in an Interior by Charles Frederick Lowcock, 1879. Among the details that characterize this Victorian setting are the tiles on the fireplace, the classical busts above the fireplace and on the pillars in the background, the circular mirror reflecting light from the window, the plant in its jardinière, and the table covered with an oriental carpet.

The most exclusive part of the house was therefore below stairs. The kitchens, scullery, butler's pantry and servants' quarters were effectively out of bounds to the family – except sometimes for the children – and certainly to visitors. This was new to the nineteenth century. At the beginning of the century it was still common practice for the mistress to take a firm hand in the running of the household. But the shift to urban living and a desire to distinguish the mistress of a household from her servants combined to encourage an infrastructure to support the home – laundries, dairies, butchers and so on. Because there was no room in a town house for a laundry or a dairy, these tasks were farmed out. In practice, of course, many a middle-class housewife did have a great deal to do with the everyday running of her household, but she took pains to conceal the fact that she had had occasion to get her hands dirty. The result was a gulf between upstairs and downstairs. The typical Victorian family was careful to avoid any association with the servants lest there be any confusion over their fragile difference in status. But those servants were the only people free to move about the whole house, though constrained by time and by their duties. In a small, middle-class house there might have been only a day servant. A bigger house would have a live-in maid who inhabited a little room at the top of the house. Yet most of her work was done below stairs. To get to and from her work the maid must have had to rub shoulders with the family. But the Victorians seemed to cope with living in such a small space. The maid had to be up long before the family, and was expected to go to bed before the family retired. She was, effectively, invisible. Thus the demarcation lines of the Victorian house were laid down – by trial, error and aspiration.

These social boundaries were reflected in the furnishing and decoration of the house. This may seem obvious: nobody expects a servant to have as sumptuously appointed a bedroom as his master. But the Victorians expressed the gradations of status with meticulous care. Guests were admitted to the best room – the parlour; this would contain the most expensive and expansive furnishings in the house, probably arranged around a marble fireplace. As you moved away from this room towards the back and the top of the house you would notice not only the furnishings and appointments shrinking and cheapening but also fixtures such as the skirting boards, plaster cornices and fireplaces. The marble fireplace would become a slate fireplace, then be reduced further to a cast iron one, until its final manifestation in the servant's room at the very top of the house – a mean little thing with a plain wood surround, designed to burn as little coal as possible. This rigidity and thoroughness is almost charming unless you are a modern-day house-owner set on knocking two rooms into one. The commonest way of doing this is to remove the wall dividing the front room from the back room. After its removal you may find to your chagrin that neither the mouldings and cornices in the ceiling nor the skirting boards around the floor match. It makes more than just structural sense to keep some of the dividing wall, either as an arch or as a frame for a set of big double doors. Then there will be some coherence to the new room.

Sometimes this fixity of purpose could be taken to ridiculous extremes in houses that were too small for the diversity of rooms required. The result was a house crammed with little boxes. But at least each room fitted the careful hierarchy of use that was so necessary to Victorian domestic living. Amongst

This morning room, photographed *c.* 1865, shows
the sort of decor and knick-knacks that were
thought feminine and suitable.

the rooms considered vital for a typical larger house would be bedrooms for sleeping, dressing rooms for dressing and washing, a study for the man of the house, a front parlour or drawing room for formal entertaining, a back parlour or morning room for the lady of the house, a billiard room, a dining room and often a breakfast room.

The idea of a front and back parlour or of a morning room may seem a trifle effete and even excessive. But the morning room was the feminine equivalent of the study. The lady of the house would use the room to instruct her servants in their day's duties, to write a few letters, to do some needlework and to entertain her friends. It was her room, and decorated to reflect her personal taste. There was a simple justification for the breakfast room, too. 'A dining room with a close, dinnerish sort of smell about it is not so provocative to the appetite as is the fresh air of a room that has not been used for eating purposes for some twenty-four hours or so,' said *The Servant's Practical Guide* of 1880. The tendency of smells to cling to the ornate and heavy hangings was well known, but there was little that could be done about them. The technological revolution arrived below stairs rather late.

Far left: There was nothing straightforward about hangings. The fashionable heavy curtains had to be 'artistic', as this picture from an 1891 advertisement for Maple & Co. demonstrates.

Left: Carpentry and Building of 12 December 1880 illustrated what it regarded as a suitable decorative treatment for a hall and stairway.

These heavy hangings were part and parcel of the twin Victorian obsessions with draughts and privacy. As any modern Victorian house-owner will testify, draughts are still a major feature. Privacy, however, was more important. The paterfamilias did not assume that the moment he stepped through the front door of his house he was on home ground and could relax. There were various stages of privacy in a Victorian house, and the hallway was the least of these. It was the first and often the only part of a house that a caller would see, so it would be decorated and furnished to impress. It often aspired to be a hall in the country house sense – rather than the mere lobby of a town house – by displaying stuffed heads, antlers and heraldic glass. V. Shaw Sparrow, editor of *The British Home Today* (1904), describes the sort of grand establishment that the middle classes tried to emulate:

Such halls form a convenient meeting place for conversation, and allow the men of the household a chance of smoking in the company of ladies instead of being relegated to the isolation of a distant billiard-room or smoke-room. The hunting man, the sportsman, are allowed in this neutral zone to intrude their bespattered clothes; and thus the hall has become again the favourite room in the house.

Stripped of his rhetoric, V. Shaw Sparrow is laying claim to the masculine nature of the hallway and to its importance for the house. The hall had to be an emphatic statement, marking as it did the boundary between the sacred home and the profane world. Even the meanest town house lobby would boast strongly coloured tiles and walls. Nicholas Cooper in *The Opulent Eye* (1976) mentions tints and combinations that are unthinkable today – lapis lazuli, orange, yellow, and even 'striped red or turquoise blue above a green dado'.

If the caller was equal to the decorative challenge of the hall he or she would be ushered into the front parlour. This room was always kept in readiness for guests, a formal room that would never be left untidy or looking lived in. Even the poorest house tried to maintain a parlour. The architects commissioned to design a certain late Victorian philanthropic housing estate for workers realized that front parlours were an impossible luxury – there was no space to spare for something so infrequently used – and they built houses that had no provision for such rooms. These sensible men were horrified to discover that the moment people moved into their enlightened dwellings they rapidly juggled around with the space alloted them until they had a room that would serve as a parlour, the family making do as best they could with the remaining space. The front parlour was obviously of prime social importance. Even today it is not impossible to find a carefully embalmed front room awaiting a guest grand enough to deserve entry.

The hall at Linley Sambourne House, with antlers on the left-hand wall and coloured glass on the half-landing.

Just as the hallway was the preserve of masculine taste, so the parlour was a repository for feminine feelings. *The Opulent Eye* gives the example of a furnishing column in *The Lady* of 1894, in which it is firmly laid down that 'the secret of a pretty room is to break up the straightness of the walls and to arrange the chairs that they look as if a merry party of gossips has only just vacated them'. That is not to say that the rooms should be unduly cluttered: 'I am hoping sincerely that my little campaign against trumpery bric-à-brac has to some extent been successful, and that my friendly readers will have begun to see the wisdom of putting aside the odd shillings they would spend on these knick-knacks until they have sufficient to buy one good thing which will be a perpetual joy.' In the line of perpetual joy the columnist suggests: 'On the table there should be a large candelabra of Dresden china. A pot-pourri bowl of old Worcester, one delicate figure, a pair of old paste shoe buckles in a faded velvet case, an antique miniature, but no more.'

In insensitive hands family portraits and a desire for 'artistic' decoration could completely overpower a room, as this 1895 photograph shows.

The first generation to document themselves in photographs were Victorians. Their frozen, sooty images have become a stereotype for the nineteenth century – a black and white stereotype. Queen Victoria's eternal affectation of widow's weeds reinforced this perception. But it was in fact anything but a monochrome century. A wander round Linley Sambourne House may persuade you that Victorian taste was both more subtle and more practical than you may have at first assumed, but it cannot reveal the true intensity of the furnishings. Curtains, upholstery, carpets and wallpaper have all survived a century of grime, London air, coal fires and cigar smoke. The tarnishing process is slow but inevitable, and all too easily goes unnoticed. One day, during a spring clean at Linley Sambourne House, some rolls of wallpaper were discovered in the back of a cupboard. The pattern was identical to the paper that had been applied to one of the bathrooms in the house, but because the spare rolls had not been exposed to light or the corrosive atmosphere they revealed the true intensity and brilliance of colours that had long since fled the bathroom walls.

In reaction to the 'artistic' interiors of the 1870s and 1880s, late Victorian

An almost stereotypical interior – solid, ornamented furniture, mirrors and paintings, long, heavy curtains and a table with a thick cover.

households were decorated in a dazzling array of strong, rich colours. In *Suburban Residences and How to Circumvent Them* (1896) Mrs Panton states firmly that

we cannot have too much real colour, and that far from demanding the timid compromises so dear to English folk, our climate and our atmosphere clamour for real sealing-wax reds, deep oranges, clear yellows and beautiful blues, and that nothing should make us temporise and have instead the smudgy terracottas, crude greens, ghastly lemons and dull greys and browns that are so liberally provided by the usual paper-hanger.

In short, the Victorians liked colour and used it freely. This, combined with a glittering array of carefully polished brasswork and mirrors under the soft pools of light from oil lamps or gas jets, and flickering in the red glow of a coal fire, created a room of richness, depth and warmth that could be almost womb-like – the ideal refuge from the brutal realities outside the front door.

Solomon Joseph Solomon's *Conversation Piece,* showing a softer, more idealized version of a Victorian interior, with a curious 'owl' sitting on the piano on the right.

On the one hand the Victorian householder revelled in the chance to make a carefully controlled statement about himself or herself and family, yet on the other was terrified lest he or she committed a simple stylistic sin to puncture the pretence. The middle classes were more interested in hard and fast rules than in letting their own taste have its way. Their own taste, once revealed, might prove too plebeian for their position in life; although, as the century progressed, 'individuality' rather than conformity became the favoured principle. The more adventurous might use as a springboard the manuals or the advice of professionals such as Mrs Haweis or Mrs Panton. But even the least confident home-maker knew that there were certain rules about decor.

The study was a masculine preserve and therefore had a more utilitarian look.

Paintings were, for instance, carefully separated into oils and watercolours, the former being said to overwhelm the colours of the latter. The drawing room or parlour would boast watercolours and tapestry – both lady-like accomplishments – while the oils, especially those still lifes of game considered conducive to conviviality and digestion, were consigned to the dining room. Reproductions and photographs of classical subjects were very common and competed on equal ground with 'proper' paintings unless they were of a slightly doubtful nature, in which case they might end up in the study. In *New Grub Street* George Gissing describes the study of John Yule:

Behind the dining room was a comfortable little chamber set apart as John's sanctum; here he smoked and entertained his male friends, and contemplated the portraits of those female ones who would not have been altogether at ease in Mrs Yule's drawing room.

Each room was furnished and decorated carefully to express its sex and function. The Victorians preferred byzantine but dogmatic complexity to ambiguity.

This concern for taste, style and aesthetic propriety was partly a side effect of the changing role of the mistress of the house. As she distanced herself from the nastier domestic chores she found herself an alternative role – arbiter of taste. It was she who would choose the carpets, curtains and furniture with which to adorn the home. This role was assigned to her partly by default; it was one of the few areas in which women could make a career. Mrs Panton, Mrs Haweis, Mrs Watson, Mrs Loudon – the list of women who were professional interior designers and who colonized the domestic interior for women is long.

There was stern opposition, of course, from leading male arbiters of taste. Lewis F. Day published a forthright condemnation of the Mrs Pantons in *Decoration by Correspondence* (1893):

The advice is always, buy! buy! buy! One sees a gleam of hope when it is suggested that a table be 'departed off' and a whatnot also 'bundled off' to leave a corner free; but it turns out that it is only to be left 'free for an easel, enamelled green, upon which your husband's portrait, draped with a golden brown scarf, might stand'. When peradventure, you are told that 'you can do without a border of any kind' it is only because 'the use of it is no longer one of Dame Fashion's inexorable laws'. Here at least there is no doubt left to us as to the teacher's criterion of taste. But for the artless reference to Fashion one would have been puzzled to imagine the point of view of those who recommended by turns a 'lovely Louis XV rose-coloured stripe' for one middle-class Victorian room, a 'cheap Moorish arch to outline the recess' in another, a ready-made cosy corner for the landing on the stairs, and a stuffed bear to serve as dumb waiter.

In *Hints On Household Taste* (1868) Charles Eastlake reserves his spleen for the 'materfamilias' who has the temerity to choose a carpet on her own.

Shall it be the 'House of Lords' diaper, of a yellow spot on a blue ground; or the imitation Turkey with its multifarious colours; or the beautiful new moiré design; or yonder exquisite invention of green fern leaves tied up with knots of white satin ribbon? The carpet is made up, sent home, and takes its chance of domestic admiration together with all the other household appointments. It may kill by its colour every piece of tapisserie in the room. It may convey the notion of a bed of roses, or a dangerous labyrinth of rococo ornament – but if 'fashionable', that is all-sufficient. While new, it is admired; when old, everybody will agree that it was always 'hideous'.

It has to be remembered that Day and Eastlake were talking to other (male) professionals like themselves – mainly architects – at a time when architects

A Victorian interior, *c.* 1860, painted by Charles Frederick Lowcock.

were trying to extend their realm to incorporate interior design. This threw them into direct conflict with the Mrs Pantons. The preface to the architect Eastlake's book is instructive:

Fifty years ago an architect would have perhaps considered it beneath his dignity to give attention to the details of cabinetwork, upholstery and decorative painting. But I believe that there are many now, especially among the younger members of the profession, who would readily accept commissions for such supervision if they were adequately remunerative, and that they might become so is evident from the fact that the furniture of an ordinary dwelling house frequently costs as much as the house itself. Of course it is possible in both cases to dispense with an architect altogether, but just as no man of real taste would entrust the design of his house to a builder, so no one should allow an upholsterer to provide its internal appointments except under advice of an architect.

Underneath all this Neo-Gothic ornament is a dining room trying to get out.

He makes clear that architects were discovering a whole new clientele in the *arriviste* middle classes. No longer should architects be content to allow a builder and his pattern book dominate the trade of creating houses. Nor should the department stores and the upholsterers and their catalogues, hand in hand with women of education but no breeding, be allowed to dictate the interior of these houses.

To justify their entrance into the arena of domestic rather than public design, architects had to have something that no woman or spec builder could possibly offer. That element was style. A trained architect was fluent in the various

idioms of the past. And so the battle of styles commenced, Neo-Gothic vying with classical exteriors, Japanese vying with Tudor interiors. Underneath all the fuss were a band of architects trying to justify their profession in the face of a small-time builder with a dog-eared copy of a pattern book in his back pocket desperately trying to avoid bankruptcy, and a Mrs Panton trying to make a living as a professional woman. This is not to say that the eclecticism of the Victorian aesthetic did not meet other needs; but the architects fired the first shot.

Various styles could quite happily co-exist within one household, each room reflecting its purpose and status rather than the personality of the household overall. A good impression of a dining room can be gained from Charles Eastlake's hearty description in *Hints on Household Taste*:

It is an old English custom to hang family portraits in the dining room, and it seems a reasonable custom. Generally large in size, and enclosed in massive frames, they

Companies like Shoolbred's offered whole rooms in a variety of styles. This one is described as a 'Drawing Room in the Louis Seize style'.

Carving the joint, *c.* 1860: a more relaxed, family atmosphere.

appear well suited to an apartment which experience has led us to furnish in a more solid and substantial manner than any other in the house. Besides, the dining room is especially devoted to hospitality and family gatherings, and it is pleasant on such occasions to be surrounded by mementoes of those who once, perhaps, formed members of the social circle which they have long ceased to join.

The implications of Eastlake's cosy little scene are that all respectable families had portraits of their ancestors. But for many a *parvenu* this was not true. They were just as much immigrants to this new class as the Irish were to a town like Liverpool. They arrived with what they could – metaphorically – carry. They had, however, the luck to ascend to their affluent new class just as mass manufacture was making many goods universally available for the first time. As a result a massive middle-class spending spree took place. For many it

A·Study·Mantel·Piece·

ROBERT W. EDIS F.S.A. AR.ᶜᴴᵀ.

Robert Edis's design for a study mantelpiece, with the masculine elements of swords, guns and armour about the fireplace and classical figures in the screen above the mirror.

was the first time they had had a status to maintain, the first time they had had money to maintain it, and the first time that the goods and services had been available to allow them to maintain it. It is no wonder that the Victorians lavished so much attention on their homes – they were their new toys.

The novelty of their position, combined with the tradition of renting property and thus being able to move at fairly frequent intervals, had implications for the way Victorians went about decorating their homes. Fitted carpets, for example, were considered an extravagance because they were unlikely to move to one's new residence. A large Turkey rug, on the other hand, fitted in everywhere, with the additional virtue that it could be lifted at frequent intervals for cleaning. The amount of money at the disposal of the house and the frequent moves made the furnishing of an entire house from new not uncommon. Catalogues of the time offered complete rooms in whatever styles were current.

Robert W. Edis, a contemporary of Charles Eastlake and also an architect, fulminated against this wholesale fickleness of taste: 'You do not, I presume,' he wrote in *The Decoration and Furniture of Town Houses* (1880), 'want to make a showplace of your homes, in which the fashion of the hour shall be exemplified in the various monotonous sage greens and peacock blues in papering. Or in quaint eccentricities of design and form in furniture and which, in a few short years, will be looked upon as crude and tasteless.' But a good number of households did exactly that. He reserved special contempt for the Victorian passion for past ages, quoting from the *Quarterly Review*:

Furniture, fire irons, teapots and the various objects of daily domestic use, made after the manner of ancients, could scarcely be turned to their legitimate purposes however well they have been to sacrifice and the ceremonies of a Greek or Roman temple. Chairs and sofas strictly made upon the model of the *sella curulis* and the bronze *bisellium* might have been comfortable in the forum, but were execrable in the drawing room. We were at last driven out of the classic mood. We could neither eat, drink, nor sit in comfort.

His idea of comfort was something solid in the Tudor or Jacobean line. Anything more recent appalled him. 'I can think of nothing more terrible than to be damned to spend one's life in a house furnished after the fashion of twenty years ago,' he said. He goes on to lambast curtains that are so ornate and over-long that they become 'the hiding place for the remains of some pet's dinner', chairs that are 'delicate' with 'the so-called "shaped" backs cut cross-grain of the wood so as to snap sharp off with any extra weight', and 'plaster ornament . . . stuck on like . . . rats on a barn door'.

The masculine abhorrence of excessive ornament may have been an aesthetic judgement, but the preference for the solidity of Tudor and Jacobean styles had a practical basis. 'We constantly hear the term light and elegant applied to a set of drawing room chairs which look as though they must sink beneath the weight of the first middle-aged gentleman who used them,' complained a middle-aged Charles Eastlake. His distaste for bedroom frills went even further.

As a lady's taste is generally allowed to reign supreme in regard to the furniture of bedrooms, I must protest humbly but emphatically against the practice which generally exists of encircling toilet tables with a sort of muslin petticoat generally stiffened by a crinoline of pink or blue calico . . . In London, especially, where dust and blacks collect whenever the bedroom window is opened, it should be avoided.

He was not exaggerating the problem, as Mrs Haweis's solution reveals in *The Art of Decoration* (1888):

Many people object to windows being much open during the summer on account of the invasion of blacks. Many years ago I tried nailing up a guard of thin strong muslin, coloured red or green, which is certainly rather useful in defeating the largest sootflakes. It should be often changed otherwise the soot with which it is charged detaches itself by its own weight.

The power that women were gaining as arbiters of style was important. It could, as in the case of Mrs Haweis or Mrs Panton, provide a profession and an income without loss of status. More importantly, it gave ordinary women an arena in which to exhibit certain 'housewifely' skills whose successes were easily displayed. Choosing furnishings was emphatically not the work of a servant. It also allowed women to go shopping.

The new department stores, such as Shoolbred's and Peter Robinson's, were springing up in and around the West End of London and its provincial equivalents to meet and encourage this new demand. They produced heavily illustrated catalogues which made shopping a much pleasanter and easier experience; previously you had purchased or ordered your furnishings from specialist upholsterers – a process not always to feminine tastes. The stores aimed not only to offer a complete range of goods and services, but also to provide a day out for their patrons, many of whom were out-of-town visitors. One genteel lady was quoted by Gavin Weightman and Steve Humphries in *The Making of Modern London 1815–1914* (1983) as saying: 'Now that the train service is so perfect between London and Bath, it is quite possible to spend a day in town and return to Bath the same evening. This is no small advantage

Whiteley's department store, Queensway, London, towards the end of the nineteenth century.

when you have a day's shopping to get through, or winter gowns and mantles to be tried on at your favourite London modistes.'

West End stores offered restaurants and retiring rooms – a euphemism for lavatories – for their customers. These splendid places were designed only incidentally for the call of nature, and became the female version of those well-established gentlemen's clubs in Pall Mall and St James's. Ladies could while away their day reading magazines, chatting with friends and comparing purchases. That is not to say that there was no practical purpose to the retiring room; it was not until 1884 that the Ladies' Lavatory Company opened the first public convenience for women in Oxford Street, and even then the convenience was apparently a source of some embarrassment to those who dared to use it. In the absence of the department stores there was little a lady of any class could do except contain herself whilst in town.

The sanitary arrangements in most homes were equally crude and, not to put too fine a point on it, smelly. Disposal of waste was a problem that grew with the burgeoning population of the city and far outstripped the few simple mechanisms the city had to cope with it. The most prevalent forms of sanitation until quite late in the century were the cess pit and the ash pit. Both had to be emptied at regular intervals, but it was not uncommon for the night soil men to arrive too late. The pit would have leaked its contents either into the well for drinking water or, worse, into the nearest cellar. A little damp was the least of the urban cellar-owner's problems during the nineteenth century. Sometimes the cess pit collapsed completely, flooding the cellar with raw sewage. Then the occupants might be forced to abandon the house, in which their places would soon be taken by the more degraded denizens of rookeries and tenements nearby, who were used to close contact with sewage. These rudimentary and fragile sanitary systems broke down completely when confronted by the density and demoralization of the slums, which always contributed heavily to the state of the streets and open sewers, already clogged with everyday refuse and the inevitable by-product of the horse – life blood of the city's transport system. The street sweeper was therefore vital – not because he attempted the Herculean task of actually keeping the streets clean, but because he could be tipped a few coins to clear a path through the refuse to allow passage from one side of the street to the other.

The Silent Highway-Man, from *Punch,* 1858, graphically demonstrates the filthy state of the Thames, at this time both London's sewer and its water source.

Right: Laying pipes. The sewage and water networks built by the Victorians are only now beginning to fail, having survived way beyond their engineers' wildest dreams.

In London things began to improve with the appointment in 1847 of the Metropolitan Commissioners for Sewers, who abolished cess pits. The Public Health Act of the following year made it obligatory for every household to have a fixed sanitary arrangement of some kind. It was the Metropolitan Board of Works, led by Sir Joseph Bazalgette, who really transformed the bemired capital into something approaching its modern state. They began laying a sewer system for London in 1859, completing the task in 1865. The rest of the country rapidly followed suit. The sewage that had polluted the drinking wells and cellars of London now poured into the Thames, turning it into a stinking, sterile mess, and it quickly became desirable to live upstream of the sewage outflows. Nevertheless the river remained a major source of domestic water.

Various forms of the flush lavatory were available, but they too smelt. The commonest type was simply a funnel running or dropping straight into the sewer. All sorts of noxious gases came straight up the pipe. Bramah's valve closet, which began life as early as 1778, dealt with this problem by fitting a complex flap at the bottom of the funnel which only opened when the closet was flushed. Even this design, however, suffered from the fault that the bowl was only properly cleaned when done by a servant. However, a smelly lavatory was better than none at all. The public convenience did not arrive until the middle of the century, when George Jennings introduced what were termed 'monkey closets' to the retiring rooms at the Great Exhibition at Crystal Palace in 1851. By 1895 he had supplied lavatories to over thirty railway companies and public conveniences to London, Madrid, Frankfurt, Hong Kong, Sydney, Buenos Aires, Cape Town and Mexico City. His earliest designs were for the space-saving underground lavatories that many British cities still have in operation. Nobody knows what he would have made of the superloo.

But it was royalty rather than Jennings who gave the biggest impetus to sanitary development. In 1861 Prince Albert died of typhoid; ten years later the Prince of Wales caught the same disease but survived. There could be no greater incentive to a Victorian for lavatorial improvement. The challenge was swiftly taken up in London by the competing firms of Crapper and Humpherson, among others. The two families lived next door to each other, in Marlborough Road, and Thomas Crapper employed two of the Humpherson brothers in his Marlboro Works. When they fell out the Crappers moved their business to the smart end of the Kings Road, while the Humphersons set up in competition at the other end.

Frederick Humpherson invented what he called the Beaufort Original Pedestal Washdown Closet. The name Beaufort came from a road near their factory – both Crapper and Humpherson christened their products after nearby roads. This washdown closet was a major improvement, for the lavatory had a U-bend to keep noxious gases at bay. This principle was not in itself an innovation; the lavatory was, however, constructed all in one piece. Previous lavatories had been composed of a separate bowl and U-bend which had to be joined up on-site, the join forming an unhygienic nook to say the least. This new lavatory was also free-standing – previous models had had to be supported in a box of some sort, adding another unhygienic cranny to the construction.

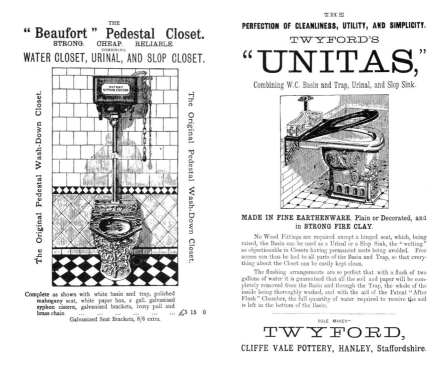

THE

"Beaufort" Pedestal Closet.
STRONG. CHEAP. RELIABLE.
COMBINING
WATER CLOSET, URINAL, AND SLOP CLOSET.

The Original Pedestal Wash-Down Closet.

The Original Pedestal Wash-Down Closet.

Complete as shown with white basin and trap, polished mahogany seat, white paper box, 2 gall. galvanised syphon cistern, galvanised brackets, ivory pull and brass chain £3 15 0
Galvanized Seat Brackets, 8/6 extra.

THE
PERFECTION OF CLEANLINESS, UTILITY, AND SIMPLICITY,
TWYFORD'S
"UNITAS,"
Combining W.C. Basin and Trap, Urinal, and Slop Sink.

MADE IN FINE EARTHENWARE, Plain or Decorated, and in STRONG FIRE CLAY.

No Wood Fittings are required except a hinged seat, which, being raised, the Basin can be used as a Urinal or a Slop Sink, the "wetting" so objectionable in Closets having permanent seats being avoided. Free access can thus be had to all parts of the Basin and Trap, so that everything about the Closet can be easily kept clean.

The flushing arrangements are so perfect that with a flush of two gallons of water it is guaranteed that all the soil and paper will be completely removed from the Basin and through the Trap, the whole of the inside being thoroughly washed, and with the aid of the Patent "After Flush" Chamber, the full quantity of water required to receive the soil is left in the bottom of the Basin.

SOLE MAKER—
TWYFORD,
CLIFFE VALE POTTERY, HANLEY, Staffordshire.

Right: The Beaufort Pedestal Closet, invented by Frederick Humpherson.

Far right: Twyford's Unitas.

This new, streamlined, free-standing lavatory was rapidly adopted in the face of the only real competition – what was called the washout closet. The washout had a lipped depression under the seat to collect your offerings which, on flushing, were hopefully swept by the force of the water over the edge, dropping with sufficient acceleration to get it all round the U-bend. The washout type of lavatory has remained popular in Germany, for some reason, but most modern British lavatories remain close to Humpherson's invention. The Beaufort, incidentally, was – like most Victorian creations – offered in descending order of quality for what the catalogue describes as 'Officers, Men, Servants and Convicts'.

Given the euphemism and embarrassment that are supposed to have surrounded the Victorian lavatory and bathroom, it is surprising to find how beautifully they were often decorated, with a wit and flamboyance that are rare today. Walter E. Mason, for example, manufactured a range of urinals which featured a life-size print of a bee under the glaze. If you remember that Victorians had a much more thorough classical education that we do today you will understand: the Latin for bee is *apis*. This flamboyance and style has made Victorian bathroom fittings very popular these days. Geoffrey Pidgeon, great-nephew of Frederick Humpherson, warns against buying original lavatories. They were made of glazed earthenware or fireclay and are much more fragile than the vitreous china of modern ones. Old lavatories, too, were usually fitted by liberal application of red lead and putty, which set solid with time. Removing a lavatory bowl that has been cemented in this way is difficult without damage. Many a lovely old lavatory has been placed in a new home, at best to leak and at worst to collapse during use because the bowl has been weakened by a crack. But do not despair. Specialist shops supply reproduction furnishings, often made from the original moulds, which look Victorian but match up to modern standards of strength and reliability.

Other Victorian bathroom ware – basins, bathtubs and so on – are more durable and equally sought after. The reasons for their introduction are ironic: one manual of the period strongly recommends having water plumbed into the dressing rooms of one's house because it was no longer possible to obtain servants who could be trusted to carry water from the kitchen to the bedroom without spilling it on the carpets. And *The Builder* of November 1879 advised its readers that 'in most dwellings there is some dressing room, or small room in a wing, where hot and cold baths can be placed, and respectable tenants will pay £5 or £10 extra rent in a moderate-sized house to secure the benefit'. Baths were what J.C. Loudon called 'a cheap and useful luxury'. That luxury was rapidly adopted. But people found that they either had no room to spare for a bathroom, or that they preferred to keep the extensive plumbing and technology at arm's length; so rather than placing it in a 'dressing room or wing' they added rear extensions to their house adjoining the stair shaft. Even today many houses of the period have their bathrooms off the staircase.

But today's bathrooms are the result, usually, of aesthetic choice. A Victorian bathroom was a simple history of its development. For example, the freestanding cast iron bathtub with its ball and claw feet now seems quintessentially Victorian. Yet it was not introduced until the 1880s. It was preceded by thinner metal baths that had to be supported in wooden cradles and panelled in, and these themselves superseded baths that were portable rather than

This bathroom suite won George Jennings of London a gold medal at the Paris Exhibition of 1889. Apart from its opulence, it boasts a pull-out bidet and concealed lavatory.

permanently plumbed in. The panelling hid the plumbing, as well as supporting the tub. The cholera epidemics around the middle of the century, which encouraged the adoption of proper toilet arrangements and 'sanitary' furnishings, also affected the bathtub. Panelled-in tubs were seen as unhygienic, and ceramic baths, which could be cleaned inside and out, became the rage. Metal tubs were, however, more suitable for households whose members liked their baths hot – a relatively late fashion – partly because they absorbed less heat and partly because of the methods of heating.

Early attempts to warm bathwater *in situ* bear a strong resemblance to a cannibal cooking pot. The logic was simple: to save hefting buckets of water boiled up on the kitchen range all the way to the bathroom, why not heat the water once it was in the bath? The Science Museum in London contains some astonishing examples of such baths: an array of gas burners would send flames licking along the underside of the bath, and only the draughtiness and chill of the bathroom saved the bather from asphyxiation or scalding. This is probably why the manufacturers recommended that the bath heaters should be removed or turned off before one entered the bathtub.

The geyser, introduced in 1869, was an improvement. It too was usually gas-fired, although other fuels could also be used. This steaming monster, resplendent in polished copper and brass, dominated the bathroom. The twin dangers of asphyxiation and scalding were still attendant on bathing, but the process seemed more controllable, and the geyser offered the best solution at the time to the problem of providing hot water to the bathroom. Circulating hot water systems such as we all have today were then in their infancy. In the mid-nineteenth century they relied on a boiler at the back of the kitchen range to propel hot water through a system of cast iron pipes that were subject to corrosion (turning the water rust red) and fracture (sometimes resulting in spectacular explosions).

THE INSTANTANEOUS WATER HEATER, or
MAUGHAN'S PATENT: GEYSER.

BATHS and LAVATORIES of various kinds.

BATH ROOMS fitted throughout.

MAUGHAN'S PATENT ABSO-LUTE GAS REGULATOR, for Gas Cooking and Heating Stoves, preventing the deposit of Carbon, &c.

THE NEW AMERICAN RETORT and other Gas Cooking and Heating Stoves, in great variety.

THE NEW and EXTRAORDI-NARY ANTI-FROST EXPAN-SION SOCKET (Lyon's Patent), for preventing Water Pipes bursting during frost.

Show Rooms, 41, Cheapside, E.C.; Factory, Cambridge Heath, E.

An 1882 advertisement for Maughan's Patent Geyser, whose main virtue seems to be an anti-frost expansion socket to prevent exploding pipes.

Although the geyser was as reliable a supply of hot water as one could expect, it had side effects: the water it supplied came out of the tap boiling hot, so steam and condensation suddenly became a problem in the Victorian bathroom. Accordingly the decor changed to cope with it. Previously it had been relatively easy to maintain a bathroom much in the style of a bedroom or dressing room – open fire, good-quality paper or paint on the walls, and polished and upholstered wooden fittings. The fireplace remained, but those surfaces that could be damaged by the moisture-laden atmosphere disappeared under a range of non-absorbent and impervious materials – slate, marble, tiles and cement. Used correctly, they gave a bathroom a faintly classical air; used badly, they made it resemble a mausoleum.

To cope with steam and to make the room hygienic, bathware became impervious and 'sanitary'.

Though carefully furnished, Victorian houses were not necessarily as cosy and as comfortable as they might seem. The coal fire is an inefficient, draughty, dirty way of heating a room. Astonishingly, some houses were equipped with central heating as early as 1800, but it was not widespread. This was partly on account of the cost and the difficulties of installing it, but mainly because it was inefficient, providing no more than background heating, and because it suffered from the same failing as all other cast iron plumbing. A frost could make the pipes explode, sending sizeable shards of metal halfway across the room. Mrs Panton was not joking when she wrote in 1895: 'No less than three boilers burst in one weekend in the place where I was staying; one resulted in the death of a servant and total blindness for the only child of the house: one in the death of three children, while the third maimed the cook for life.' Loudon's *Architectural Magazine*, more concerned with aesthetic aspects, said: 'It is earnestly hoped that the hot water mania may never expel our ancient, cheerful and wholesome open hearth from our dwellings; if so, we may expect to see the ruddy English cheek supplanted by the bleached and kiln-dried aspect of our Continental neighbour.'

This 1892 fireplace was no ordinary hearth: the small print tells us that it has a central heating apparatus. The advertisement recognizes the contributory effect of coal fires on London's atmosphere.

Coal fed that wholesome hearth, fired the central heating, burned in the kitchen range, powered the steam engine and was the raw material for gas and for coal oil. Coal was the rich black heart of the nineteenth century, cheap enough to waste:

The enormous waste of fuel may be estimated by the vast cloud which continually hangs over this great metropolis, and frequently overshadows the whole country, far and wide; for this dense cloud is certainly composed almost entirely of unconsumed coal, which having stolen wings from the innumerable fires of this great city has escaped by the chimnies and continues to sail about the air, till having lost the heat which gave it volatility, it falls in a dry shower of extremely fine black dust to the ground, obscuring the atmosphere in its descent, and frequently changing the brightest day into one of more than Egyptian darkness.

This horrifying picture of smut-encrusted London had been painted by Count Rumford in 1796, but things got a great deal worse once the industrial revolution was in full swing. Spurred on by the wasteful black future of London, the American-born Count – his title was Hanoverian and his real name was Benjamin Thompson – invented the improved fireplace. It was smaller, more efficient in combustion, drew better and threw more of the heat of combustion into the room rather than up the chimney. By the 1850s most houses had Rumford-style fireplaces, not just for reasons of economy – coal was cheap, after all – but because efficiency always appealed to the Victorians.

Barrow Steelworks, painted by G.H. Andrews in 1874, gives some indication of what is meant by industrial quantities of atmospheric pollutants. This was what caused the notorious 'pea-souper' fogs of Britain's industrial cities.

Nowadays the Victorians have a reputation for euphemism, evasiveness and decoration for decoration's sake. But just as the retiring rooms of the department store seem at first a typical expression of those characteristics and on closer examination turn out to be almost wholly practical and certainly good for business, so there is a strong pragmatic streak running through most Victorian design. It was, admittedly, allied to a love of fakery. They delighted in passing off an item or a material as more expensive than it really was. This was

practical in a sense, since they were making best use of a cheap material.

Take plasterwork: you could say that it was used by the Victorians to supply ornamentation that might, in more expensive houses and earlier times, have been provided by carved stone or wood. Yet there was often a very practical reason for the use of this cheap and flexible material. At Linley Sambourne House, for example, the ornate ceiling roses are pierced to allow the fumes from oil and gas lamps to escape into vents concealed behind the roses and be ducted into the street. This was a Georgian device that relied on a gap between floor and ceiling. Late Victorian houses do not have enough of a gap for such ducting. Decoratively sand-blasted windows seem quintessentially Victorian, combining as they do a love of glass and of embellishment. But the opaque glass also offered the practical advantage of admitting natural light without loss of privacy. It presents yet another example of an aesthetic object fulfilling a peculiarly Victorian utilitarian role.

Victorian paintwork developed out of the eighteenth-century habit of trying to make cheap wood look more expensive by scraping a grain in the wet varnish. Standing next to some examples of this work at the Victoria and Albert Museum in London are some nineteenth-century panels painted with virtuosity by a gentleman named Kershaw. Only by looking very carefully at the edges of the panels can you tell that their surface appearance has nothing to do with the material of the panels themselves. Kershaw's work was displayed at the Paris Exhibition. The chauvinist French raised an outcry, claiming the panels on show were a fraud – that they were not painted but merely skilfully veneered. Kershaw, sent to Paris, asked for a panel of deal and a panel of slate; in front of his challengers he painted the deal to look like marble and the slate to look like fine wood. The French awarded him a special medal.

Not all Victorian marbling and graining was up to Kershaw's standards. It was an extensively practised technique, much abused, and there are as many bad as good examples. Take a look at the next marble Victorian fireplace you encounter and try to guess, without touching it, whether it is real marble or merely slate or cast iron painted up to resemble marble. It does not seem to have bothered the Victorians that this kind of gilding the lily should have been obvious. Lighting was of course less bright in a Victorian house than it is now, so you could get away with some fairly crude approximations. Perhaps the techniques of marbling and graining were most enjoyed by the Victorians because they relied on the observer only seeing the surface of an object. They themselves often did not wish to be honest about their own origins, and it may have given them a taste for surface appearances in their furnishings as well. Middle-class manners and a 'marble' fireplace could get you a long way.

Acid-etched or sand-blasted glass allowed the light to enter a room, but created an effective barrier to prying eyes or unsightly back yards. The most exuberant designs were usually applied to the doors and windows of pubs.

The improvement to the Victorian house which pushed it into the twentieth century was the introduction of incandescent lighting. The oil lamp had not been noticeably better at casting light than a candle, nor had the gas jet been much brighter than an oil flame. In fact the installation of a gas system was almost more trouble than it was worth. The pipes that supplied the gas to the burners had to be inclined at a slight angle, so that the water vapour which condensed in the pipes would drain down to a point at which it could be siphoned off, rather than impeding the efficiency of the burners. All three forms of lighting caused smoke and fumes and cast only a very gentle light. In photographs of the houses of the day the furniture is arranged in little huddles around the various light sources. The first advance was the incandescent gas mantle, which arrived in the 1880s. When heated by a gas jet the mantle glowed white-hot, emitting a great deal more white light than anything that had gone before. At about the same time the incandescent electric bulb also arrived. This operated on the very similar principle of heating an element inside the glass envelope until it shone white-hot.

The arrival of efficient light in the Victorian home made night as bright as

An 'artistic' late Victorian interior by Liberty's with a frieze of peacocks, a typical motif.

day. For the first time it was possible to see the other side of the room after dark. The Victorians looked at their rooms under the harsh scrutiny of this new light and found them cluttered and ugly. No longer flattered and given depth by gentle pools of light, the rooms had to change. A taste for simplicity and relative sparseness in furnishings developed, helpfully coinciding with the Arts and Crafts movement. The charm of marbling and graining melted away once you could see how it was done. The conjurer was exposed.

The Welsbach incandescent burner.

4. Exteriors, Gardens and Beyond

To a middle-class Victorian the city began and ended at the front door – the world was the home writ large. The shops and tradesmen who supplied the house were an extension of the kitchen and the servants. Even the public parks were just models for the domestic garden. This may seen a rather selfish world view, but the late twentieth century has some equally odd notions about the Victorians. You can see the consequences on any tastefully restored Victorian house: glossy black railings, creamy white stucco and white window frames – a black and white reincarnation of the Victorian house owing more to monochrome photography than to historical veracity.

Apsley House, once the London home of the Duke of Wellington, is now a museum to the Iron Duke, housing his trophies, uniforms and decorations. A few years ago the Victoria and Albert Museum were asked to advise on the restoration of the exterior. The household accounts of the estate contained frequent references to the painting of the imposing railings that run along the front of the house. But according to the accounts the railings were painted green – bright green. Paint samples taken from the railings themselves showed this to be true. Until the 1940s the railings had been coloured an eye-searing blue-green. Off came the black gloss and, based on the V & A advice, on went a green so potent that when the railings became due for painting again the contractors suffered a loss of nerve, opting for a faded green that matched the railings after they had weathered for a few years. The Apsley House railings are still green, but not quite as historically verdant as they should be. Nevertheless they are a welcome change from the glossy black and municipal green railings that hem in the rest of Hyde Park Corner.

Cast iron allowed designs for almost anything to be produced easily and cheaply. Any resemblance to expensive wrought iron was entirely intentional.

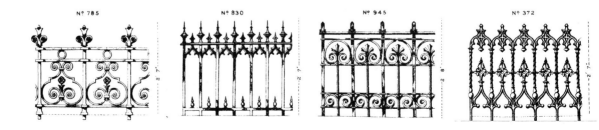

N° 785   N° 830   N° 945   N° 372

A flat-fronted Georgian-style terrace with arched windows, fanlights above the front doors, painted stucco and painted railings. The frontage is dressed with flowering plants as per Charles Eastlake's recommendations.

The logic behind these green railings is quite simple. The Victorians liked their interior decoration to look more expensive than it really was – embossed wallpaper dressed up as plaster or wood, grained cheap woods masquerading as expensive woods, slate or cast iron pretending to be marble, chairs in the Chippendale style and so on. They took a similiar approach to exteriors. To start with, to have any sort of control over the look of the outside of your house showed that you were no ordinary tenant. And in a society that took face value at face value, façades were extremely important.

The nineteenth century felt great reverence for the classical world: an educated gentleman was supposed to be fluent in Greek and Latin language, literature and culture. And any man who aspired to be a gentleman would wish to demonstrate his learning in these fields: in the Greek and Latin tags strewn through a lot of Victorian writing (although the habit is not confined to that century), in the affection for classical inscriptions about their homes, often accompanied by the portrayal of some mythical figure or an appropriate deity from the pantheon, and even in the '*Salve*' on the doormat. It is also the reason why the Apsley House railings are green. The Victorians thought that if railings had been Greek or Roman, they would have been made in a particular style – which the Victorians aped – and they would have been made of bronze rather than plebeian cast iron. Few could afford real bronze railings – although there are some examples in Paris and New York; instead, they painted the railings to look like bronze. Bronze rapidly patinates into a bright, powdery blue-green, the result of reacting with the atmosphere. The atmosphere in Victorian times was particularly reactive and rapidly oxidized any exposed metals; hence the fashion for classically styled verdant green cast iron railings.

Similar aspirations governed the painting of window frames. Most frames today, irrespective of period, tend to be painted white. The Victorians did not have the sophisticated array of paints we are used to. Their colours still tended to be earth-based, although the brilliance and strength of aniline dyes were beginning to make an impact. The water-based paints were basically distemper – that is, lime with a bit of colour added – and consequently rather powdery, with little or no ability to stand up to the weather. The oil-based paints were limited in their range of colours since the oil and the atmosphere or sun reacted with some of them. Blue, for example, remained a fugitive hue until quite late in the century. White – today's choice – was problematic. Uncoloured distemper would give a lovely off-white finish to an interior – except that white rooms were for most people out of fashion and impractical in the soot-laden atmosphere of the coal-fired industrial revolution. When applied to the exterior of the house oil-based white paints were, like other oil-based colours, subject to atmospheric pollution, degradation by the sun and discoloration from the linseed oil on which they were based.

Pugin's winning design for the new Palace of Westminster after the fire of 1835 helped set the fashion for Gothic Revival. But one of his classical allusions was to specify bronze – not for the railings, but for the window frames. Though expensive, it was quite practical. Bronze does not corrode in the way cast iron does – the verdant patina protects it from any further oxidation – and it does not warp or rot like wood. It thus became fashionable to paint window frames the colour of patinated bronze. It made quite a picture – green window frames, perhaps green-painted cast iron around the window boxes or balcony on the first floor, and green railings at street level. It looked expensive, fashionable, tasteful and fake – and was commonly laid on a canvas of equally fake stone-coloured stucco.

This lapidary illusion depended on a combination of workmanship and paint. Victorian paint quality was uneven: because it was mixed on-site there was

A typical façade with classical portico and ironwork. Unfortunately, however, painting the window frame on one side of the front door a different colour from the other has upset the balance of the terrace.

little consistency between the paint at the top and the bottom of the bucket, let alone between different batches of paint. The modern DIY decorator expects in these days of quality-controlled emulsions to be able to produce a wall of flat, even colour with the wave of a roller. To do this in Victorian times was the work of a skilled decorator who was constantly modifying his materials and methods to suit the weather and the surface he was painting. He was rarely expected to produce a flat wall of a single colour. The friezes and dados, the ragging, dragging, marbling and graining were all techniques much in demand, and all either depended on or ignored the patchiness of the paint. The same was true for the exterior. It was the very patchiness of the paint that helped stucco look like stone. It is hard to visualize those stucco frontages impersonating stonework now that so many of them are covered with gloss paint the colour of clotted cream. Victorian stucco would have been painted to match the local stone. In Bath, for example, it would have been a lovely honeyed pink to match the real sandstone buildings. In London things were much duller: Portland stone, the colour of wet cement, was the vernacular building stone used there.

So the exterior of the real Victorian house was far removed from its modern-day black and white impersonation. The window frames would be anything but white: if not bronze-green they might be grained to simulate oak – oak being considered the queen of woods (and also the most expensive). The

Evening in a London street. An enormous number of gas jets were needed to light the shop windows.

railings would not have been black. And the stucco, though perhaps a dull grey, would often be enlivened by picking out in a contrasting colour the incisions meant to represent mortar. Any Victorian terraced house exhibiting this colourful ostentation today can, and does, get criticized as being anachronistic – a criticism better levelled at the soot-and-clotted cream school.

The twentieth-century vision of a Victorian street is perhaps conditioned less by photographs of the period than by period films: a black and white Basil Rathbone striding through the fog-shrouded streets of London, cobblestones gleaming fitfully in the gaslight; or the technicolor all-singing, all-dancing Oliver pocket-picking his way into a life of crime in the exotic slumberworld of the

Pear Tree Court today. These Peabody Trust dwellings of forbidding aspect replaced the slums described by Dickens in *Oliver Twist*.

Artful Dodger and his pals. Film companies may seem to spend a fortune on their product, but like any enterprise they spend only enough to achieve what they hope will be a decent return. Authenticity is taken only so far, and re-creations of the last century usually economize on one main essential – dirt. Dirt is expensive to apply and remove to locations and extras. It causes problems of continuity, and it can distract the audience from the business in hand of identifying with the protagonist. Sherlock Holmes is somehow less impressive wading ankle-deep through horse manure, and Oliver is certainly a lot less photogenic when surrounded by the lice-infested spawn of the rookery, survivors of typhus and cholera. Hans Zinsser's biography of the plague bacillus, *Rats, Lice and History* (1934), records that during the second half of the nineteenth century 'transmissible diseases were, of course, still plentiful; and scarlet fever, diptheria, meningitis, and measles – which had been previously masked to some extent by the more rapidly spreading and violent contagions – now attained greater prominence.'

Dickens was trying to show the middle classes what they were closing their front doors to – slums, disease and degradation. In *Oliver Twist*, published in 1838, he placed Fagin's den in Pear Tree Court off Farringdon Road in London. Later this most notorious slum was redeveloped by the Peabody Trust as low-cost housing. It still exists opposite the *Guardian* building in Farringdon Road: a mean little close with a forbidding frontage of scrubbed London stock that even today causes a shiver. The streets of the Victorian cities were not places to stroll and linger. A range of criminals that would astonish even the most ardent law and order politician today lay in wait to commit anything from a garotting: ('He attacked from behind and without warning, slipping a rope or cloth or simply a powerful arm about the victim's neck, and with vigorous strangling pressure forced him to bend back. Meanwhile his partner quelled any attempt to struggle by blows against the helpless man's exposed front as he rifled his pockets,' as Kellow Chesney described it in *The Victorian Underworld*, 1970), to a 'kinchin lay', explained with relish by Fagin: 'The kinchins, my dear, is the young children that's sent on errands by their mothers, with sixpence and shillings; and the lay is just to take their money away – they've always got it ready in their hands – then knock them into the kennel and walk off very slow as if there's nothing else the matter but a child fallen down and hurt itself.' It was often the only way to survive in a nether world where a living wage was rare.

Then there was the traffic: thousands of horses, carts, carriages and cabs clogged the streets. The oats and hay that went in one end of the horse inevitably emerged at the other end, somewhat more adhesive and odoriferous for the experience, and added to the refuse underfoot. A shower of rain was all that was needed to turn a thoroughfare into a lake of liquid manure. The only thing to be said in favour of street refuse is that it helped deaden the incessant clatter of iron-shod cartwheels and hooves on stone cobbles. The modern rush hour is sedate by contrast: pneumatic tyres on tarmacadam make little noise, and the steady rumble of competing internal combustion engines can seem almost soothing when placed against the infernal din of screeching cartwheels, whinnying horses and shouting cab drivers. It was no wonder that straw was laid outside the houses of the sick in an effort to mute the awful racket. There had to be a quieter alternative to cobblestones.

In 1838 David Stead patented a form of tar-soaked wood paving, followed in 1839 by Robert Carey's system of interlocking blocks of wood and stone. With true Victorian empiricism an experiment was embarked upon that year to find a better road surface. Twelve companies each laid a section of paving in London's Oxford Street – wood, asphalt, bitumen, granite etc. As a result of

A nineteenth-century traffic jam.

the experiment Carey's system was adopted for paving certain London streets. The stone preserved the wood longer than it might otherwise have lasted on its own, but added to the noise. It was not until 1871 that an improved version of the system, employing wood alone, was introduced to Bartholomew Lane. This was rapidly adopted elsewhere, so that by 1884 there were 53 miles of London streets paved in wood – mainly creosoted Baltic deal. Poking through holes in the tarmac of the car park at County Hall in London, vestiges of these wooden cobbles can still be seen.

The Victorians were nothing if not optimistic. They could always improve on their world, as they could always improve upon themselves. The compensation for the loss of the measured social structures and supports of the eighteenth century was a nineteenth-century freedom to make oneself anew. The road to self-realization was paved with education. There were books, night classes, workers' institutes, public lectures and specialist societies all purveying education, which effectively become a major recreational pastime for the Victorians.

The other recreations of drink and religion were important in the development of the new suburbs. Cash flow was always a problem for builders, and there were various ways of easing this difficulty. Houses could be offered to prospective purchasers before they were built. But purchasers demanded rather more than just a map and an artist's rendering of the finished product;

A typical grouping of terraced houses and pub.

they wanted to be certain that they were buying into a respectable area. So the first thing a sensible builder or developer erected on a new estate was a church. The cheapness of gin and the drop in the price of ale and beer during the nineteenth century had led to an explosion in drinking matched only by the fervour of the temperance movement. The artist George Cruikshank, a leading teetotaller, achieved fame with his moralistic anti-drink cartoons bearing titles such as *The Drunkard's Children* (a skilful combination of Victorian obsessions)

A Cruikshank cartoon designed to speak for itself.

and *The Bottle* (which sold over a hundred thousand copies within days of publication) – but to very little effect. Pubs grew faster than the cities – as much the result of the building practices of the period as of any sudden expansion in national thirst. The second edifice the spec building put up on any new estate was always a pub. A speculator would build a pub, install a landlord and take a cut of the profits. It gave the workers a place to slake their thirst, it gave the wily builder a place to pay out the weekly wages, and it gave the publican first bite at the workers' wage packets. As fast as he paid out wages, the builder got them back across the bar – and stayed solvent a little longer. But the situation could sometimes go too far, as *The Builder* reported in 1854:

On the pastures lately set out for building you may see a double line of trenches with excavations on either side . . . and a tavern of imposing elevation is standing alone and quite complete, waiting for the approaching row of houses. The propinquity of these palaces to each other in Camden and Kentish Town is quite ridiculous. At a distance of two hundred paces in every direction, they glitter in sham splendour.

The idea of a virgin site dotted with marked out foundations but boasting nothing above ground except the startling combination of glittering pubs and glowering churches has very practical roots: they were vital to the financial survival of the builder.

Right: Small private enterprises could flourish in Victorian times: (*above*) coffee and dining room; and (*below*), a butcher's shop.

Below: A street of nineteenth-century shops and services, including a pub, a man's outfitters, a coal office and an undertaker's.

There was little legislation controlling the development of these new estates beyond the often haphazard strictures of the landowner. A modern-day planner may feel that a community centre or a shopping mall are needed to breathe life into a new estate: the Victorian developer relied on demand creating a supply of small shops and businesses to support his new suburb. There were plenty who wanted to go into business on their own account. Small shopkeepers could, under the right circumstances in these hothouse cities, grow rapidly. Shoolbred's expanded from a tiny shop to become a department store dominating Tottenham Court Road in London from the 1860s until the 1920s, when the family were able to sell up and become landed gentry – the perfect success story. Everybody was looking for an opening to get themselves started, and in some ways it was an ideal time to be a small shopkeeper. There were no supermarkets to compete in the field of the basic necessities. Transport was such that everyday shopping was done very locally. Only the big department stores in the West End of London and in other great cities aspired to stocking to meet every possible whim of their customers. Most shopkeepers were specialists. In 1868 an ordinary high street in Stoke Newington, North London, boasted a brewer, a wine merchant, a fruiterer, an oilman, a pawnbroker, a linen draper, a chemist, a dentist, a whip manufacturer, a piano tuner, a cheesemonger, a brushmaker, an upholsterer, a marine store, a gas fitter, a hairdresser, an undertaker, a bookseller, an umbrella-maker, a surgeon, a solicitor, an insurance agent and the ubiquitous offices of the Imperial Gas, Light and Coke Company.

There was a network of shops and services supporting the Victorian house – stables, coal merchants, dairies, carpenters, decorators, builders and servants. Managing tradesmen was a skill second only to managing servants in the middle-class house. In *The Diary of a Nobody* Mr Pooter records the preliminary skirmishes after he and his wife Carrie had moved to a new house:

April 4. Tradesmen still calling: Carrie being out, I arranged to deal with Horwin, who seemed a civil butcher with a nice clean shop. Ordered a shoulder of mutton for tomorrow, to give him a trial. Carrie arranged with Borset, the butterman, and ordered a pound of fresh butter and a pound and a half of salt ditto for the kitchen, and a shilling's worth of eggs. . . .

April 5. Two shoulders of mutton arrived. Carrie having arranged with another butcher without consulting me.

April 6. Eggs for breakfast simply shocking; sent them back to Borset with my compliments, and he needn't call any more for orders.

April 9. Commenced the morning badly. The butcher, whom we had decided not to arrange with, called and blackguarded me in the most uncalled for manner.

Those trials drove Mr Pooter to his diary. Some householders would have taken solace in religion, self-improvement, drink or opium, all of which acted as distractions from a life that was often miserable and short. In the crowded, polluted cities mortality, especially amongst children, was appallingly high. Victorian society rose magnificently to the task of celebrating that mortality. The middle classes especially welcomed a chance to display their wealth, taste and respectability. Funerals were spectacular, and funerary art rose to heights unequalled today. The minutiae of what to wear, when to wear it, permissible behaviour, souvenirs of the departed and so on reached almost necrophilic heights during the nineteenth century. It was a way of mourning the passing of a dear one at the same time as celebrating one's own continuing existence. As ever, there were manuals on how to do it – correct down to the tiniest blossom: 'There are many flowers that speak to me of early happy death,' wrote Charlotte Elizabeth Tonna in *Chapters on Flowers* (1836).

The lily of the valley is one: but the fairest is the white moss-rose. . . . The pall may spread its velvet folds and the sable plumes bow in stately gloom over the dead; but a single white rose, drooping amid its dark foliage, tells the story more touchingly, with more eloquent sympathy, than all that the art of man may contrive, to invest in sorrow in a deeper shade of woe.

The burgeoning population of the Victorian city pushed up the death rate to astonishing heights, the inhabitants of the city being so concentrated that a place to bury the dead was at a premium. Some were never buried. Victims of pestilence were often carried away in the night lest those in contact with the victim be ostracized. Families too poor to be able to give their child a proper funeral and too ashamed to endure a pauper's grave for their loved one would abandon the tiny corpse in the steets.

But there were also too many legitimate corpses. As early as the 1820s several London churchyards were reported to have upwards of 3000 corpses per acre, and by 1843 the 150 graveyards of London contained an estimated 50,000 putrefying bodies. The air was dark with vapour. In *London in the Nineteenth Century* (1909) Sir Walter Besant quotes a Dr Walker's description of St Sepulchre, Snow Hill:

With a population including Middlesex of 13,500, it has two 'slips' on either side of the church, which together can if at all exceed a quarter of an acre. There are vaults under the church; but if anyone, having perceived the effluvia some yards from the open door, can descend, unimpelled by duty or private feeling, he has stronger nerves than the writer's, although sorely taxed in this troublesome world.

Lucinda Lambton writes in *Vanishing Victorians* (1976) of corpses being gouged out of the earth, sometimes only weeks after interment, chopped up with axes and saws specially kept for the purpose, thrown into charnel or bone houses and left to rot, sometimes even to be sold for manure. In short, the cemetery was an appalling place, a cess pit of mutilated and partially decomposed bodies fighting for space. It was time for a change.

New cemeteries were laid out along scientific lines. The architect John Claudius Loudon planned his churchyards to give corpses enough room: each coffin was to be buried 6 feet below the surface – it was not uncommon for shallowly buried coffins, propelled by the gases of putrefaction, to rear up through the recently replaced sods – and 6 feet from any other grave. Trees were planted to soak up the water that was a by-product of decomposition and to prevent the graveyard turning into a noxious swamp. Art, of course, went hand in hand with this new science. In his succinctly titled work *On the Laying Out, Planting and Managing of Cemeteries; and on the Improvement of Churchyards* of 1843, Loudon wrote that these places

properly designed, laid out, ornamented with tombs, planted with trees, shrubs, and herbaceous plants, all named, and the whole properly kept, might become a school of instruction in architecture, sculpture, landscape gardening or arboriculture, botany, and in those important parts of general gardening, neatness, order and high keeping.

Redemption through education and self-improvement was his message.

Loudon's vision became a common reality, and the Victorian cemetery a thing of splendour. Stripped of its corpses it also made an excellent public park, combining the opportunity of airing the working classes with the space to erect improving statues and memorials instead of gravestones; Victorian parks and cemeteries are very similar in appearance.

Left: Highgate Cemetery, London, in the mid-nineteenth century, not long after it was opened.

Right: Highgate Cemetery as it is today.

This wonderful edifice, presented to Victoria Park in London by the philanthropist Angela Burdett-Coutts as a drinking fountain, can still be seen today. But most of the mouldings have been damaged, the statuary vandalized and the plumbing ripped out.

The Victorians had a passion for monuments, spurred on by a campaign in *The Builder* in the 1840s which resulted in the creation of, amongst other souvenirs of past glories, Nelson's Column in Trafalgar Square. The paper rather ungraciously dismissed it as 'a great stick or wand laid across a picture and always marring the view of it'. The taste for the monumental could take a more practical turn, again campaigned for by *The Builder* (it did after all mean work for the trade), in the form of the drinking fountain. You can still find them in older parks, rather sad, lonely edifices – the extremities of the statuary snapped off by generations of vandals, the classical inscriptions obscured by graffiti, the plumbing long since ripped out for scrap, the whole having an abstracted air, the site of midnight courtship and a daytime rendezvous of mothers and prams. The erection of these fountains in the late 1850s was encouraged by the combined forces of the temperance movement and the town planner. The reasoning was simple. Benjamin Scott, quoted in Lucinda Lambton's *Vanishing Victoriana*, told a temperance meeting in the City of London:

Many of our citizens complain that they cannot find a wholesome substitute for beer or other drink; and I think the suggestion of having water fountains in London is a good one. . . . One day I saw in Cornhill eight or ten people waiting at the pump there to drink; and it struck me that fountains or pumps in the streets would save men from drunkenness.

The Builder heartily endorsed these sentiments:

To those who doubt whether such a movement as this will tend to diminish drunkenness we would only say this – consider the fact that literally thousands quench their thirst in the course of a single day at only one of Liverpool's fountains; can any sceptic be so credulous as to believe that all these thousands, were there no such fountains, would carry their avowed thirst past the pot-house, and go home to tea or dinner as it might be with blood as cool and as free of alcohol as by the quenching of their thirst at the fountains?

While houses were erected all about at the whim and speculation of builders and developers, parks were assembled with care and attention to the needs of the populace. Regents Park in London and Birkenhead Park in Liverpool were financed by the construction of the houses either in or overlooking them. Birkenhead Park, designed by Paxton in 1843, became the inspiration for Central Park in New York. Many Victorian elements survive in municipal parks today: serpentine walks, ornamental lakes, monuments or statuary, perhaps a bandstand or aviary, a shrubbery and bedding plants. This pattern, developed for the cemetery and refined in the park, transferred itself, almost wholesale if not whole-scale, to the domestic garden. It relied on three developments dating from just before the Victorian age, that are in themselves simple but in combination changed the face of parks and gardens across Britain.

The first of these was the Wardian case. Dr Nathaniel Bagshaw Ward had a passion – not uncommon among Victorians – for ferns, but his ardour was frustrated by the corrosive air of London that killed every plant it touched. Taking them into the house was no help either, since the fumes from the oil or gas lamps were equally deadly. Then in 1829 the doctor discovered that his beloved ferns not only survived, but flourished with very little attention, if sealed in a large bottle. By extension, he found that a glass case created an artificial environment in which greenery could survive without additional water or attention for remarkably long periods of time. Variants of this Wardian case can still be seen in certain well-preserved Victorian houses. Linley Sambourne House has some attractive ones – rather like glassed-in window boxes

One of the glassed-in window boxes, based on the Wardian case, at Linley Sambourne House.

protecting the plants from the poisons of the inner and outer atmospheres whilst encasing them in their own micro-climate: an ideal way of coping with the city. Beeton's *Book of Garden Management* (1872) said:

Many years ago we accepted an invitation to visit a gentleman living in the very centre of the densest part of London, – a square in which Mr Dickens has placed the Cherrible

Brothers, and their factotum, Tim Linkinwater. . . . Here we found every window occupied by a glass case, in which plants were growing in a manner which astonished us; ferns of the greenest and freshest hue; orchids, such as we have rarely seen surpassed, were growing there, redolent of health and vigour; and we were told, to our great surprise, that the cases were hermetically sealed, and no water had been administered for many months. This was the first we had seen of the Wardian cases, since so celebrated.

The true worth of the Wardian case was not in its domestic application, however. As the Empire expanded, so did the role of the plant-hunter. Before Dr Ward, exploring botanists were resigned to 90 per cent of their samples dying *en route* to Britain. Crossing the tropics was sufficient to kill all but the hardiest temperate zone plant, and the final chilly leg of the journey usually did for any tropical plant. What the climate did not destroy, the salt from the sea spray was happy to finish off. The Wardian case changed all that. But to take advantage of the treasure house of exotic plants offered by the case, British

This large glasshouse gives an idea of how a conservatory was used – lots of mirrors, dark wood, palms and ferns.

nurserymen and gardeners needed to use another recent advance – the glasshouse.

Modern tourists being rushed through the orangery at Versailles find little time to reflect on its purpose. There is barely enough light to grow a moss, let alone an orange. Versailles was constructed when it was still thought that all a plant needed to survive a winter was warmth. The discovery that light

Even without its jungle, a Victorian conservatory is still an impressive sight today.

massively improved a plant's life expectancy was put together with the technology for construction using the new cheap glass. The glasshouse had come of age. It enabled the skilful gardener to extend his growing season and to provide controlled climates to suit more fragile plants. It allowed him to nurture the strange new growths brought from the other side of the world in Wardian cases. And it meant that these plants could be propagated and given a head start on the seasons, so that they were in their prime when the time came to plant them outside.

The Victorian park could be kept in constant bloom by this method. Bedding plants were reared under glass, bedded out as they came to bloom and then replaced once past their best – a common form of municipal gardening even today. The Wardian case and the glasshouse offered the Victorian gardener a large and growing vocabulary of cheap and healthy plants. But the domestic garden needed one further development – the lawnmower.

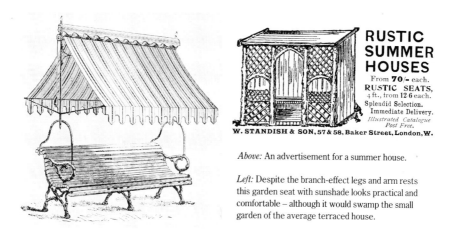

RUSTIC SUMMER HOUSES
From **70/-** each.
RUSTIC SEATS,
4 ft., from 12 6 each.
Splendid Selection.
Immediate Delivery.
Illustrated Catalogue
Post Free.
W. STANDISH & SON, 57 & 58, Baker Street, London, W.

Above: An advertisement for a summer house.

Left: Despite the branch-effect legs and arm rests this garden seat with sunshade looks practical and comfortable – although it would swamp the small garden of the average terraced house.

In the days of Capability Brown, in the eighteenth century, only grand houses had had gardens in the ornamental sense. In fact what they had were landscaped parks, which swept right up to the edges of the house. Within that park there might be specialist gardens – one for vegetables, one for topiary, one for roses, one for herbs and so on – but otherwise you stepped from the house into the park. The grassy sward was kept at bay by flocks of sheep or by teams of men wielding scythes. Neither method produced anything like the green lawn we think of as grass these days. The old adage of the perfect lawn being sown, rolled and watered for several hundred years is far from the truth: the concept of the English lawn is barely a hundred years old.

Then in 1830 Edwin Beard Budding signed an agreement with John Ferrabee, an engineer, for the manufacture of a machine for 'cropping or shearing the vegetable surface of lawns, grass plots or pleasure grounds'. He had invented the lawnmower. Or rather he had applied to a new use a machine originally designed to shave the nap off cloth. In any event, the lawnmower came into being. Early illustrations show the mower being dragged by a team of men, probably the same ones who used to do the scything. There were also horse-drawn and steam-powered mowers. But very rapidly the team of men shrank down to one, and that man rose steadily up the class scale until the catalogues displayed a mower intended to be used by gentlemen. There is even reference to the mower being suitable for ladies. The result was a democratization of the domestic garden and the creation of a new middle-class pursuit that remains in the affection of the British to this day.

Like the municipal park, the early nineteenth-century domestic garden boasted a great deal of statuary, serpentine paths, a small lake or pond, bedding plants, ferns, a monkey puzzle tree, a rockery and some exotica as a conversation piece making up the rest of the pattern. Loudon coined the term 'gardenesque' for this scaled-down version of the Picturesque. Sometimes the scale was so reduced that the serpentine path became a short and frantic wriggle of eccentric intensity. To modern eyes this kind of garden may seem excessively cluttered, but to the Victorians it was a reaction to the sparse and orderly arrangements of the eighteenth century combined with the modern advantages offered by newly discovered species of plant and new gardening techniques. But it is true to say that mid-Victorian embellishment of the garden treated it more like another room of the house than as arable land. There was rusticated furniture of almost every kind, constructed either of unbarked thinnings of wood or of wrought iron in the style of branches. A vast range of ornament was available – statues, sundials, vases in cast iron, imitation marble or artificial stone and even, as J.C. Loudon describes in his *Encyclopaedia* (1834) 'stone or cast iron mushrooms, painted or covered with moss, mat or heath'. It can be assumed that the voluminous garments regarded suitable for women of the time went some way towards protecting them from spiky garden furniture. But a feminine presence in the garden also prompted Charles McIntosh in his *Book of the Garden* (1853) to aim a barb at 'pretended connoisseurs who object to statuary altogether, unless clothed with more than a fig leaf . . . we may answer "honi soit qui mal y pense." '

Even the larger garden suffered by its impersonation of a park. 'An Amateur' wrote in *The Gardener's Magazine* of 1828 that such gardens 'hold forth every inducement to wander among their groves and lawns, and gaudy flower-beds;

Conservatory, urns and serried ranks of plant pots down the steps convey the Victorian idea of gardening.

they are captivating at first sight; they are beautiful in fine weather'. But in bad weather

do dripping shrubs, do wet grass, and swampy ground, and flower-beds, known only as beds for flowers by their dingy mould, contrasted with the yellow lawn, do all, or any one of these, invite us into the open air? . . . The first and chief object of a pleasure-garden being thus, throughout the greater portion of the year, denied to us.

This 'swampy ground' was sometimes the consequence not only of horticultural excess but also of arable indulgence. Mrs Loudon, writing in *Gardening for Ladies* (1840), said:

Now, the fact is, that . . . most small gardens have been manured a great deal too much; and in many, the surface soil, instead of consisting of rich friable mould, only presents a soft black shining substance, which is the humic acid from the manure saturated with stagnant water. No appearance is more common in the gardens of street-houses than this, from these gardens being originally ill-drained, and yet continually watered; and from their possessors loading them with manure, in the hope of rendering them fertile.

Such conditions made the conservatory all the more attractive. In 1845 the tax was lifted on glass, just as its quality was beginning to improve. Sir Joseph Paxton, basing his design partly upon the leaf structure of *Victoria regia* (properly *V. Amazonica*) – a gigantic South American water lily which he had coaxed into flower – created the biggest conservatory of all, the Great Exhibition building which became known as the Crystal Palace. Everybody had to have a conservatory until it became a Victorian cliché, feeding off a fancy for novelty. Nurserymen were happy to meet the demand; in *The Practical Gardener and Modern Horticulturalist* (1830) Charles McIntosh listed coffee, sugar, cocoa, sago, chocolate, Jesuit's bark (cinchona), cinnamon, ipecacuanha, balsam of capivi, cassia and gum arabic seeds and plants. Not only were these a challenge to grow; they also had an educational purpose.

The statuary arranged around the garden was, by its classical allusions, meant to have a similarly pedagogic influence. In the 1880s Sir Charles Isham introduced a miniature population of statuary in his rockery of alpine plants.

That energetic horticulturalist, the late Mr Loudon, having been impressed with the value of such an adjunct when tastefully introduced, idealised, forty or fifty years since in one of his ponderous volumes, a group of children under some specimens of *Pinus nanus*, adding remarks on the beauty and interest such a treatment might add to gardens. What delight would the realisation of the idea have afforded him, especially the Gnomes.

Thus wrote Sir Charles in *Remarks on Rock Gardens, also Notes on Gnomes.*
The garden gnome had arrived.

The mid-Victorian garden was a very artificial thing. *The Cottage Gardener* of
September 1856 points out that

nothing is more easy than the planting; the great art is in the training, the cutting and
carving, which must be constantly looked to throughout the season, to keep every
shoot, leaf, and flower as if the whole were turned out of a band-box, or as the
lady's-maids look after the hair, the dress, and the *fal-dals* of their profession. Without a
constantly lady's-maiding, a flower garden would soon look as rough as Polly Hopkins.

And just as such a manicured garden was a reaction to the eighteenth century,
so the Arts and Crafts movement of the late nineteenth century reacted to such
busy gardens. From about 1890 the cottage look became fashionable for small
gardens – a wooden butt for rainwater, a trellised porch and simple wooden
furniture in plain oak or elm. In larger properties Gertrude Jekyll, a disciple of

The Victorian public park
developed from the Victorian
cemetery to become a
fashionable place for families to
exercise their children and meet
their friends.

the New Landscape School, encouraged arches and pergolas. William Robinson, the leader of the movement, suggested a simple summer house which had the additional benefit of being a place to which children could be banished. Sundials were still favoured. But geometric bedding-out was replaced by herbaceous borders filled with perennials. Terraces, arbours, clipped hedges and gravel walks gave way to grass, rustic steps and 'shrubby clumps'. The skill of a fashionable late nineteenth-century garden now resided in the planning rather than in the formalized layout.

Despite statuary, gnomes and exotic plants the garden often had a practical side, though it tended to be the prerogative of the rich and the poor and bypassed the suburban villa. A modest cottage garden would be used mainly to grow vegetables and fruit to supplement the meagre budget for food. At the other end of the social scale only the well-off (earning at least £2000 a year, according to *A New System of Practical Domestic Economy*) could afford the permanent gardener needed to maintain a kitchen garden. The range of

The outdoor staff that were needed to manage gardens of any size – in this case the grounds of Erddig in Wales.

produce was astonishingly wide. Seed catalogues early in the nineteenth century list not only a spread of varieties but also vegetables that were later to be regarded as exotic – capsicums, globe artichokes, garlic, borecole (kale), salsify and scorzonera. Unfortunately the techniques for preparing the produce of the garden were not equal to the task: boiling to the point of extinction was the commonest solution. But even the most urban suburban garden had some aspirations to self-sufficiency. In *The Diary of a Nobody* Mr Pooter recorded:

> *April 9*. Planted some mustard-and-cress and radishes, and went to bed at nine.
> *April 11*. Mustard-and-cress and radishes not come up yet.
> *April 12*. Mustard-and-cress and radishes not come up yet.

And then, with finality:

> *April 14*. I procured and sowed some half-hardy annuals in what I fancy will be a warm sunny border.

Whatever its size and pretensions, the Victorian garden, like the rhododendron and the herbaceous border, set the pattern for our modern gardens. And of course it complemented the Victorian house in supplying yet another area of specialized refuge from the world outside.

Note: The authors acknowledge the use in this chapter of material in *The Victorian Garden* by Tom Carter (Bell and Hyman, 1984).

5. A Home Fit for Living

On a clear winter's night in London you can smell a crime being committed. A solitary plume of smoke, obscuring the frosty stars, points at a chimney, scenting the air with the authentic Victorian bite of rolling yellow fog. A fireplace is being reintroduced to the forbidden pleasures of soft coal. The Clean Air Act does allow you to feed your fire smokeless fuel, but this is a pale substitute for the cosy glow of the authentic high-tar brand. Alexandra Artley and John Martin Robinson's guide to the conservation way of life, *The New Georgian Handbook* (1985), says that a fire gives a room focus – 'cats, friends and crumpets know *exactly* where they are' – and supplies purpose to a conservation lifestyle: 'Mr New Georgian gets up at dawn to pay the coal man, clean out the ashes, ring the sweep, delve into the cellar, *light* the fires, rub up the grates (NG men compare notes about Zebrite, now sold in tubes) and nip out for a packet of Zip.'

Despite their name, New Georgians are mostly New Victorians, though they range, claims the book, from the 'Soanies' – Neo-Classical romantics living in derelict Bloomsbury terraced houses *c.* 1820 (and named after Sir John 'England's greatest Neo-Classical architect' Soane) to 'Kentucky Fried Georgians' who live in 'a very select Georgian-style development' *c.* 1987. Mid-Victorian taste translates as 'Liquorice Consort': 'More is more. Guests can't stand it for long. There is pastel, wishy-washy chintz, delicate wax things under domes, the alarmed face of taxidermy, Nottingham lace curtains, a Belgian black marble fireplace with two scrolls . . . ' and a great deal more.

The fireplace was an essential element in the Victorian house and remained so, despite the mess and draughts it caused, until the post-war craze for boarding up. Encouraged by DIY magazines and television programmes, thousands of fireplaces and staircases disappeared beneath chipboard and plywood, leaving houses 'streamlined' (now pronounced 'boxy') and covered in white gloss paint. The walloping increases in the price of oil during the 1970s and the long winter power cuts, encouraging householders to think seriously about alternative forms of heating; a growing nostalgia for the 'authenticity' of the nineteenth century after the grand failures of post-war planning and architecture; and the more recent fashion for paying lip service to 'Victorian

The hall of William Morris's Red House, Bexleyheath, Kent.

values', have all combined to create a resurgence of interest in 'original features' such as the fireplace.

In effect this has created three kinds of Victorian house: the Mausoleum, the Mimic and the Modern. Mausoleums – houses that have survived *virgo intacta* from the last century, and which have become templates for the Mimic – are few and far between. Linley Sambourne House, the jewel in the crown of the Victorian Society, is a fine example. The unanimity and domesticity of the house, as well as its density of ornament and intensity of colours, can persuade the most hardened sceptic to express a grudging admiration for the period.

The Mimic (often a Liquorice Consort) lives in a house that has been restored to its original Victorian state, or, more commonly, to a Victorian style. It is fashionable. to imitate the middle classes of a century ago, conveniently ignoring the role and style of the poor, exploited working classes. Many a nineteenth-century artisan's cottage is now dressed in middle-class Victorian clothes. There are, however, enough people who get it right to prevent mimicry seeming ridiculous. The trick is to reflect the period and the status of the house accurately without subsuming your own tastes and lifestyle.

How to damage the look of your Victorian house. . . .

Essentially you need a good knowledge of your house and of the period, and you have to be accustomed to a fairly formal lifestyle; in other words no children.

Most people, however, compromise with the present and modernize their Victorian house to a certain extent. The Modern house has all the utilities we take for granted, such as central heating, and often many of the 'original features' – fireplaces, cornices and so on. The degree to which the 'Victorian-ness' of the house survives depends on the inhabitants. But just as the Victorians looked to previous ages for inspiration, we look to the Victorians; and, like theirs, even our most accurate and reverential impersonations are an expression more of our own age than of the model.

Linley Sambourne House is in the centre of the imposing façade of Stafford Terrace, a quietly expensive street just behind Kensington High Street in London. When it was first built it was merely middle-class: now it seems sumptuous and impressive. There is a small brass plaque on the front door to tell callers whether the Sambournes were at home or not, the lettering barely decipherable after more than a century of polishing. The Mimic's house cannot boast this kind of verisimilitude and makes do with a knocker of the appropriate style – an acanthus leaf design in brass or iron, perhaps complemented by an ornate letterbox (the penny post was introduced in 1840). The Modern house has a doorbell.

In case the plaque was not enough, there was always a servant in attendance to field and filter callers – normally the job of the parlourmaid. It was an important role: Mrs Linley Sambourne specified that, when the parlourmaid was busy dressing, the housemaid should take her place and 'Answer Hall bell until 20 past' as well as coping with her other tasks: 'Hot water jug filled in mine and spare room, basins wiped. My bed arranged for resting.' It was all part and parcel of sustaining a solid façade against the world. The *cordon sanitaire* was respected. Mrs Beeton's *Book of Household Management* (1859–61) states firmly:

In all . . . visits, if your acquaintance or friend be not at home, a card should be left. . . . If paying a visit on foot, give your card to the servant in the hall. . . . The form of words 'Not at Home' may be understood in different senses; but the only courteous way is to receive them as being perfectly true.

There is no servant to protect the Mimic from unexpected callers, nor indeed for the Modern household. The Modern house, however, does have an equivalent of the maid with an ear cocked for the telephone – the answerphone. Not quite as decorative as a maid in livery, it nevertheless allows the householder to be out to double glazing salespeople but at home to friends. On the other hand, the answerphone is by no means as widespread today as servants were a century ago.

The true differences between the three types of houses – Mausoleum, Mimic and Modern – can be seen once you manage to get inside the front door. A genuine nineteenth-century house is imposing from the start, and the restored house aims to exude the same degree of dense decoration. But while a Victorian householder could obtain the materials and furnishings as a matter of course from the upholsterers, decorators or one of the new department stores, the Mimic's home is a triumph of painstaking detective work and bargaining. The true Mimic began reconstructing his (Mimics seem to be mainly male) house long before it was fashionable, when all about him were engrossed in the headlong rush to 'modernize'. All he needed was a practised eye and a little patience (as well as a thick skin) to pick up most of the essentials in Victorian decor and furnishings. Now that fashion has caught up with the Mimic, the discarded Victorian fireplace free for the taking is but a memory. The inevitable middleman now asks a respectable sum for such an artefact. There are specialists in old fireplaces, old wood, old brick, old slate; in plaster, wallpaper, paint and furnishings. Any householder with sufficient money can avoid months of obsessive grubbing through skips and demolition sites, days optimistically wasted at auctions and hours spent cultivating dealers in antiques and junk. Everything you could possibly want can now be bought off the shelf. It costs more and, for the purist, it's a lot less fun. It is also an area where a little knowledge can be a dangerous thing.

Nowadays a growing range of architectural salvage companies sell the bits they garner off building sites. They range from the charmingly named House Hospital in Battersea to the massive Solo Park – 3 acres of secondhand bricks, tiles, slates, timbers, stone, doors, windows and innumerable little bits of ironmongery whose original purpose has long been forgotten except by the select few – stuck out in the middle of the Cambridgeshire fields miles from anywhere. The true Mimic cries real tears at the sight of a decent array of architectural salvage. And because of the localized nature of building materials until quite late in the last century, as well as the various vernacular building styles, the items needed for your house are likely to be found close by.

The source of knowledge (and sometimes of architectural salvage) about the Victorian house is the Mausoleum. If it survives, study it: if it is being demolished, salvage what you can. The Mausoleum of Linley Sambourne House is now a museum, but was once a functioning house – and the way in which it is decorated and furnished shows this. An ornate ceiling was one of the focal points of the room because the lamps cast so much light on the ceiling. The only source of heat (which also provided some of the light) was the coal fire. The first-floor sitting room of Linley Sambourne House has not one but two ornate fireplaces, and the furniture and furnishings are arranged to take account of the twin needs for light and warmth. Dim lighting and the focus of a fire are essential to the look of a Victorian room.

This can leave the Mimic in a bit of a quandary. He can go to the ascetic extremes of Californian Dennis Severs, who has martyred himself for the sake of his eighteenth-century house in London's Spitalfields, a totally authentic reconstruction, burning ninety candles each night for light and old packing crates for heat. Alternatively the Mimic can compromise – flame effect gas

The first-floor sitting room of Linley Sambourne House with its two marble fireplaces. The density of the pictures would have seemed a little excessive even in the house's heyday.

fires instead of the real thing, low wattage bulbs in period fittings, and perhaps – if he is bold enough – the sybaritic luxury of central heating. To the purist the purpose of central heating is quite acceptable in a reconstructed house. The problem is the form. Central heating engineers invariably place radiators in exactly the wrong place in a room. One of the essential features of the Victorian arrangement of furnishings was balance. The mass of the fireplace was balanced by an equally large lump of furniture on the opposite wall, a central window was matched by a facing doorway or mirror, and the ornamented ceiling rose was reflected in the circular pattern of the rug below. There is no room for radiators in this arrangement, especially since most engineers would place the main radiator exactly where the big sideboard that balanced the fireplace was to go. The skill with which the mechanics of central heating can be concealed in such a room exercise the ingenuity and imagination of the Mimic greatly. The Modern house, on the other hand, can happily combine a white marble fireplace and immaculate cornices with fitted carpets, central heating and a mixture of old and new furniture. All it takes is taste. The Mimic's house needs the combination of taste and historical knowledge tempered with the practicalities of heating, lighting and plumbing.

Decorative metal bands for holding back heavy Victorian curtains.

One of the most striking features of the Mausoleum is the zest and confidence with which it was furnished. It is hard, as many a Mimic has found, to combine that confidence with a painstaking accuracy of the period. The danger of seeming over-reverential is always present. The Modern house has no hard and fast rules on fashioning an interior, and aims merely to be itself – which often means that it should do nothing but attempt to reflect the personality of the owner as modulated by current fads and fashions. It is not unlike the Mausoleum – though perhaps a little less colourful – and it is the furniture that tells the story.

The Mimic's house is one of many that benefited from the tail end of the great furniture cull that began with the introduction of incandescent light in the final years of the last century, turning rooms of mysterious depth into overstuffed and cluttered parlours. As the twentieth century progressed, more and more Victorian furniture found its way into junk shops or antique shops.

A true Victorian interior has potted palms, *objets* under glass, and heavily patterned wallpaper as a backdrop for paintings, prints, photographs and knick-knacks.

There was a lot of it around, the consequence of mass production meeting the masses in the mid-nineteenth century. The Victorians always aspired to seem one stage better than they were. The rich could afford to buy genuine pieces of furniture in whatever the fashionable style was. In *The Opulent Eye* Nicholas Cooper describes how the middle classes tried to follow suit: 'This generally meant furniture that valued apparent costliness above authenticity, and room arrangements that made up in the quantity of objects what was lacking in quality.'

Certain elements in these imitations were favoured – the bandsaw and wood-carving machine made carving a relatively cheap aspect of the impersonation of old furniture. Styles that relied on carving for their personality were pushed – Chippendale, Jacobean and so on – rather than Continental styles that depended on expensive inlay or embroidered upholstery. One writer welcomed the wood-carving machine, saying: 'Anything which tends to make homes artistic, without any great expenditure, is to be welcomed with enthusiasm.' The furniture firms were happy to cash in on a salesman's dream – a potent combination of the middle-class hunger for the 'artistic' with the middle-class ignorance of style. A trade paper in 1892 noted that: 'Twenty-five years ago the average customer would rather have weighed a chair than consider its particular style.' Many of these 'artistic' impersonations are still with us. John Fitzmaurice Mills and John M. Mansfield offer a warning in the foreword to their book on fakes, *The Genuine Article* (1979):

Much of genuine Chippendale furniture was too austere for the taste of Victorians: such knowledge makes it easier to tell the difference between a real Chippendale chair and a Victorian fake. The Victorian piece is nearly always a trifle over-decorated with heavy carved embellishments which, although they are unlikely to fool many today, were exactly what the nineteenth-century buyer was trying to find.

While a Victorian house may have been furnished entirely with 'new' antiques, the Mimic's house will be a judicious (one hopes) mixture of those 'new' antiques and modern reproductions, and the Modern's a sparser and more eclectic mix of perhaps an inherited antique or two, some junkshop pieces and a smattering of modern furniture. Despite current opinion, which derides reproduction furniture, there may well be one or two 'repro' examples as well. While a blatantly overdone nineteenth-century Chippendale pastiche can be amusing, it should not be forgotten that modern reproduction furniture can be astonishingly bad. Take the now fading fashion for stripped pine: demand outran the supply of old pine furniture and encouraged the 'creation' of reproductions in nineteenth-century styles with a 'stripped' finish to them. The final stage of this exploitation of the genre was 'pine' chests that are actually chipboard covered with paper printed or embossed with a wood grain. It makes Victorian graining look like high art.

The real difference between the Mausoleum and house interiors today is one of confidence. Both contemporary houses are seeking a solution to a crisis of confidence in design. The Victorians, in the middle of a love affair with science and engineering, at the height of their powers, worried only about what the neighbours would think. Design was either 'artistic' or the solution to an engineering problem. The British today have an equal lack of confidence, but in design. Aesthetic qualities are seen as something extra, to be added to an object to help sell it: it is not a means of making an object more functional or easier to use. To furnish your house you either compromise with a mixture of old and modern, or you go the whole hog for the oldest affordable period when there was still a confident and recognizable 'style'. It was Georgian, it is now Victorian, and it is becoming 'Thirties Chic'.

The fashion for Victoriana is partly a function of the cheapness of antiques relative to modern furniture. A Victorian sideboard may cost a couple of hundred pounds – more if it is a good piece of work. A modern sideboard of comparable quality in materials and workmanship can be priced at a thousand pounds or more. A lot of prospective buyers prefer their furniture secondhand, and they also feel safer with secondhand taste.

The Italians are often held up as the antithesis of tentative British taste. Their aesthetic heritage is, if anything, greater than ours but it has not intimidated them. Instead, with an eye educated by daily contact with the kinds of art and architecture a tourist hopes to see once in a lifetime, they demand an object of utility that also pleases the eye. Italians are used to finding even the most banal object available in a pleasing form. The British expect the banal and the mundane to look banal and mundane. God forbid they should relish the colour of a plastic bucket. The Victorians had this zest, relish and self-confidence. The ancient Romans never made coal scuttles – but the nineteenth century could do a pretty good impersonation. How about a vivid red Turkey carpet? Make sure it is made in Birmingham rather than Bombay, though. 'The crimson used in Scinde rugs, for instance, is especially destructive, and the portions dyed with this colour wear out long before the rest,' warned Charles Eastlake in *Hints on Household Taste*. The real orient was less trustworthy than the British imitation.

Most Modern householders are synthesists: neither bold enough nor rich enough to create the world anew, they devote their energies to modifying the world they have been given. The house of their Victorian forebears is accepted

Above: Wallpaper designed by William Morris for Compton Hall, Wolverhampton, *c.* 1890. As was quite common, the Compton design was also printed on chintz.

Above right: A Walter Crane design for a wallpaper frieze.

as the basis for a twentieth-century lifestyle. It mixes old and new: a log-effect gas fire in an old fireplace, reproduction bathrooms with modern plumbing (and yes, there are Victorian bidets), and modern paints to replicate old techniques.

The real Victorian house depended on cheap labour for its decoration and maintenance. The density of its furnishings and the speed with which they got dirty in an age of coal fires, oil or gas lamps and a soot-laden atmosphere demanded constant scrubbing, dusting and polishing by a battalion of servants. A foreigner visiting an English house of the time was astonished: 'The English houses are like chimneys turned inside out; on the outside all is soot and dirt, in the inside everything clean and bright.' Without servants the process was rapidly reversed. Yet servants were seen as a burden rather than a boon to the master and mistress of the house. Mrs Beeton's *Book of Household Management* notes that

It is the custom of 'Society' to abuse its servants, – a *façon de parler*, such as leads their lords and masters to talk of the weather, and, when rurally inclined, of the crops, – leads matronly ladies, and ladies just entering on their probation in that honoured and honourable state, to talk of servants, and, as we are told, wax eloquent over the greatest plague in life while taking a quiet cup of tea.

Mrs Beeton observes that since servants depend on the goodwill of their employers the bad domestic is the exception, bad masters and mistresses being more often the source of trouble.

Most of the domestic cleaning fell to the housemaids. They were supposed to rise between six and half past six in the morning. 'Earlier than this', says Mrs Beeton, 'would probably be an unnecessary waste of coals and candles in winter.' The maid would then do the living rooms downstairs: opening the shutters, cleaning the fires, polishing the grates, laying and lighting new fires, moving all the furniture to sweep the carpet, moving all the bric-à-brac to dust the furniture and finally dusting and polishing that bric-à-brac – all this before laying the table and serving breakfast to the family. If she was a maid-of-all-work, her cleaning duties were almost unending. Cleaning plate and knives before the introduction of stainless steel was an unpleasant everyday task. The maid's thumb would soon be raw from rubbing jeweller's rouge (or even brick dust) into knife blades to polish them. It is no wonder that Mrs Beeton advised that 'if there are many ornaments and knick-knacks about the room, it is certainly better for the mistress to dust these herself, as a maid-of-all-work's hands are not always in a condition to handle delicate ornaments'.

The maid-of-all-work was at the bottom of the servants' hierarchy – often the only servant a household could afford; hence Mrs Beeton's reference to the mistress doing the dusting. The bigger the house, the wider the range of servants. Lord among servants was the butler. He delegated as many of his more menial duties as the number of available servants allowed. He supervised the serving of meals, he hired and fired male servants, he managed the silver and the cellar, and, in company with his female counterpart, the housekeeper, he ruled the house. As a security measure his bedroom was often next to his pantry in which the silver was stored. In grander or older households he would be responsible for brewing the beer that the servants drank. He was also in charge of the wines of the house, ordering barrels which he would fine, bottle and cork. Insobriety, a common failing in butlers, was probably one of the reasons that the master of the house took an increased interest in the management of his cellar as the century progressed.

You could hear the housekeeper coming: the symbol of her office was the châtelaine of keys attached to he waist. Her status in the house rose with the arrival of the Victorian middle classes, more and more of the everyday running

The housekeeper and her minions.

of the household being relinquished by the mistress and dropping into the lap of the housekeeper. As the butler had his pantry, so she had her store cupboard – in which she waged constant war against vermin. Floor and grains were kept in containers on hanging shelves; loaf sugar was wrapped in paper and hung from a hook; tea was kept in a lead-lined chest; and coffee, once ground, was placed in a tightly sealed canister far away from anything else so that it should not get tainted.

The mistress had control over the butler and housekeeper, who in turn managed the male and female servants respectively: the footmen, valet, cook, kitchenmaids and housemaids. The exception to this was the nursemaid. She was an anomalous figure in that she usually came from a slightly better background than the rest of the servants, and the nursery was usually some distance from the rest of the house. She was given charge of children as soon as they had been weaned until about the age of five, when they began to spend mornings in the schoolroom with a tutor or governess. This was the point at which boys stopped being dressed as girls and were 'breeched'. Since around a quarter of children born in the mid-nineteenth century failed to reach the age of five, breeching was an important event. Child mortality may perhaps in part be explained by the treatment meted out to children. Mrs Beeton gives the following recipe for a tonic to encourage convalesence after measles:

> Take of infusion of rose leaves, 6 ounces.
> Quinine, 8 grains.
> Diluted sulphuric acid, 15 drops.
> Mix.
> Dose, from half a teaspoonful up to a dessertspoonful, once a day, according to the
age of the patient.

When she was not poisoning her charges the nursemaid was expected to be handy with her needle, skilled at ironing and trimming little caps as well as keeping both children and nursery clean. Dust and dirt were no respecters of status, although in larger households the nurse might be able to delegate cleaning to an under-nursemaid.

Today's lighting and heating do not create the dirt of their Victorian counterparts, and late twentieth-century skies do not, on the whole, rain cinders. It should be easier to keep a house clean these days. The Modern house, sparsely furnished by Victorian standards, and equipped with all mod cons, requires far less maintenance. But the frequency and expertise with which the house is cleaned depends entirely on the skill and time of the householder. Few have the time and/or the expertise to scour the house thoroughly each day, and even fewer can afford to pay somebody to do the job for them. It is possible that today's houses are dirtier than their nineteenth-century counterparts. The Mimic's house has the biggest problem, for nimble-fingered housemaids are few and far between. A room so densely furnished that there is barely space to swing a vacuum cleaner can hardly take advantage of the modern technology that has replaced those maids. With truly Victorian concern for appearances, it is often only the most visible surfaces that stay clean.

Although advances in Victorian domestic technology lagged behind those in industry there was a great deal going on below stairs. The kitchen still looked

Above: Booth's Trolley-Vac, 1906. It was connected to the light fittings – wall plugs came later. The clean patch of carpet is meant to have just been vacuumed.

Right: Gas and electricity took some time before they matched the utility and efficiency of solid fuel.

Far right: The permutations on the basic kitchen range were almost infinite.

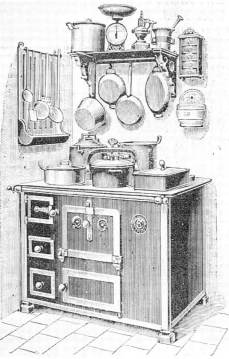

fairly primitive – black-leaded ranges where now there would be a gleaming white split-level cooker – but there were inklings of change. The advent of mass production allowed the cook an entire *batterie de cuisine* where before she had had to manage with a few dented pots and pans. Early food processors (the Science Museum in London has one dating back to 1850), apple corers, cherry pippers, knife polishers, carpet sweepers (invented by Bissell in 1876), and finally, towards the end of the nineteenth century, the vacuum cleaner, all seem signposts leading the way to the well-equipped modern fitted kitchen. But the real modernization had already happened – in the ingredients used in the kitchen.

Despite all those homely recipes in books and manuals of the period for black lead, glue and silver polish, it was a time of commercialization for many of the commodities used in the home. Anything from custard to boot polish could now be bought rather than made, and early examples of bottling and tinning began to alter the Victorian menu radically. Until successful means were invented of preserving meat – either in carcass or on the hoof – and vegetables, midwinter food had been less than appetizing and strong, spicy recipes were commonplace. (Tinned meat, introduced from Australia in 1874, was christened in Navy messes 'Sweet Fanny Adams', after an unfortunate lady who had been hacked into steaks by her lover.) But once it became possible to obtain meat and vegetables fresh and wholesome enough to serve undisguised, the British diet began on its insipid Heinz 57 varieties road to gastronomic limbo. The almost Indian ferocity of pre-Victorian cooking still survives in dishes like devilled kidneys.

Few working Victorian kitchens survive. Even the most diehard Mimic has to eat, and the idea of firing up a bad-tempered black-leaded range every morning for the sake of a cup of coffee rarely appeals (especially now you can't get real black lead – it's too poisonous – and the substitute just won't shine). The Modern Victorian house is usually happy with a wooden plate rack as a nod in the direction of the past. The real question that separates the Mimic from the weekend restorer is not what is in the kitchen – since many a Mimic takes the sensible view that few Victorian visitors ever saw the kitchen, and so his own can be equally out of bounds and therefore merely functional – but where to put the kitchen. In a smart eighteenth- or nineteenth-century town house the kitchen was relegated to the basement, keeping noise and smells at an arm's length from the main body of the house. A less imposing establishment may have had its kitchen in the back extension or even in the back room on the ground floor. Modern living has integrated the kitchen with the rest of the living space. It demands that the kitchen be moved up the house to a more convenient position, on either the ground or first floor, and becomes a palace of high-tech fittings. The Mimic will probably keep his kitchen in the basement – despite its somewhat gloomy aspect – as a way of maintaining the fiction of a dark, malodorous, servant-strewn under-stairs.

On the other hand, both the Modern householder and the Mimic are crazy about Victorian bathrooms, partly in reaction to the mean-spirited thing that the modern mass-produced bathroom suite has become. They may be all the colours of the rainbow, ergonometrically accurate, economical in water usage and cheap to buy, but the flatulent sound of wet flesh sliding around a plastic bath somehow detracts from the pleasure of a solitary soak. There is no need to spend a fortune on an old cast iron tub on four claws, and yet a further fortune having it re-enamelled. There are modern bathrooms of material, size and style to make bathing a pleasure. A large proportion of them just happen to resemble the Victorian originals – if you can ignore the jacuzzi embedded in them. A well-seasoned original or reproduction mahogany lavatory seat is infinitely to be preferred over a modern plastic one. A four-square washbasin with a lip to prevent water slopping out of the front is both more practical and more lovely to behold than a cheap modern peach- or avocado-coloured scalloped basin whose sole purpose seems to be to funnel water down the front of the user.

These modern reproductions of Victorian bathroom fittings give an idea of the quality now available.

When these expensive Victorian bathroom fixtures are compared with cheap, bottom-of-the-range modern ones it is no wonder the Victorian bathroom suite seems attractive. But the comparison is false. Just as a Victorian artisan's terraced cottage should not now be dressed up to look like a middle-class suburban villa, so that cottage's bathroom (a relatively recent acquisition) should not be modelled on something that even the suburban villa was unlikely to have. The twentieth-century view of the nineteenth shares the latter's propensity for playing fast and loose with reality.

The real differences between the Mimic and the Modern householder emerge when it comes to adjuncts of the house that did not exist in any form in the last century. The Mimic is unlikely to have anything to do with double-glazing, for example. Current opinion endorses this. It is more cost-effective to insulate the loft of a nineteenth-century house (for which a grant may be available) than to double-glaze it. If – because of a noisy neighbourhood, for example – double-glazing is still considered necessary, conservationists recommend secondary glazing as being less damaging to the appearance of the house – as well as being cheaper. Any amount of insulation and secondary glazing will not, however, keep a Victorian house warm. In the last century noxious fumes given off by oil or gas lamps demanded well-ventilated rooms, and open fires ensured a steady draught through the house. The Victorians protected themselves, to a certain extent, from the steady breezes playing about their home by the use of screens, heavy curtains and hangings. Whether they realized it or not, those chilly zephyrs actually had a useful purpose – apart from coping with lamp fumes, they also swept away the moisture either condensing on or seeping through the solid walls.

Today's careful householder, heedful of frequent campaigns exhorting him or her to 'Get more for your Monergy' may find that draughtproofing causes more problems than it solves. Elimination of the sub-gale force winds playing about the house may reveal remarkable problems of damp and condensation. More worryingly, draughtproofing can lead to a dangerous level of air pollution within the home. In 1986 the Building Research Establishment issued a publication entitled *Domestic Draughtproofing; Ventilation Considerations*, in which it says that even cursory draughtproofing can cut the efficiency of gas fires or cookers, as well as reducing the amount of air available to dilute waste gases, resulting in sometimes fatal concentrations of carbon monoxide. Such concentrations kill about two hundred people in Britain every year. For this reason, and because the Institute of Health Officers now believes that the resultant condensation is a health risk, neither kitchens nor bathrooms using gas appliances should be draughtproofed. The BRE further recommends that homes recently insulated with urea-formaldehyde foam should not be draughtproofed for at least a year, although, they say, 'there is no evidence available to suggest that draught-proofing can lead to formaldehyde related problems'.

Even without the dubious aid of draughtproofing, many contemporary owners of a Victorian house have discovered rising damp. Modern homes protect themselves against moisture climbing their walls through capillary action by means of a damp-proof course – between the foundations and the walls there is an impermeable membrane to keep water at bay. Damp-proof courses were required in all houses built after 1875, but often these have worn out or been bridged; 'bridging' merely means that some material has made a link between the brickwork above the damp-proof membrane, connecting it to the damp ground. Concrete plinths designed to conceal the DPC or flowerbeds running along the foot of the walls of the house are common culprits. But if the DPC has failed, or never existed, then either a new DPC will need to be inserted or other action taken to prevent damp climbing up the house. Classically, a new DPC is inserted in much the same way that foundations are infilled. A portion of the wall is shored up, a course of bricks removed, new bricks and a DPC put in their place, then the whole procedure repeated on the next section of wall, and so on. This process can, however, be speeded up by using a chainsaw to cut a continuous slot in the mortar joint of the wall. Any imaginative house-owner will have an idea of how expensive such heroic action can be. The alternative treatment is alleviation rather than cure – either by silicone injections or through a series of porous tubes that are arranged in the affected wall to drain moisture out of the brickwork before it can do any damage. The effectiveness of alleviation varies.

Today's householders, confident of the structural integrity of their houses, are often tempted into extending the living space upwards or backwards. The back extension has honourable Victorian and Edwardian antecedents; a nineteenth-century model for a loft extension is rarer. Modern building regulations are far more extensive and demanding than their nineteenth-century equivalent and it is they, in part, which govern how such expansion will fit in with the rest of the house. For example, regulations require a minimum ceiling height of 2.3 metres (about 7 feet 6 inches) for at least half of a sloping-roofed attic. A dormer window is the easiest way of achieving this in a loft conversion – and the quickest way of destroying the look of a Victorian house. Consequently many planning authorities object to dormer windows. But what they will not be able to see after it is installed they do not object to; many dormers are concealed on the side of the roof not visible from the street. It is possible to meet room height requirements by lowering the ceiling joist that

There are many ways of putting windows into a Victorian house.

will form the floor of the extension – a lot of work. Once sufficient headroom is obtained, by whatever means, the room in the loft can then be lit by a roof window. This is a modern vision of the skylight, lying flush with the roof and doing less damage to the overall appearance of the house. Planning authorities may still insist that such windows are not visible from the road.

With back extensions, the main areas of difficulty are likely to be the foundations, the brickwork and the roof. Building regulations may require deepening of the foundations of the house where it adjoins the extension. The extension will need cavity walls, causing difficulty in matching the brick bond with the original structure, and even if the bonding matches the bricks may differ in size, colour and texture from the old ones (see p.41). A flat roof covered in bituminous felt is a common sight on extensions because of its cheapness, but it destroys the uniformity that should exist between the house and extension. Apart from the aesthetic damage caused, this kind of roof has a tendency to suffer from water penetration and damp rot. A lean-to pitched roof not only looks better on a Victorian house, it also throws off rainwater more easily and, because of its better ventilation of the roof space, has less chance of developing rot.

In a perfect world every house would conform to these simple but sometimes expensive guidelines. The difference between reality and perfection is sometimes governed by ignorance, but more often by money. With sufficient funds it is possible to do wonderful things with any house. The challenge comes from doing as good a job practically and aesthetically as is possible with a given house and limited resources. The final judge of the success of such an enterprise is not the historian nor the architect, but the person who has to live with it.

6. A Buyer's Guide

The average Victorian house is not an antique: it is neither old enough nor rare enough to be treasured in quite that way. Instead, the Victorian house is quietly becoming an endangered species. A fourteenth-century cottage, on the other hand, can fetch a good price these days just because it is old. In the right place it can be a remarkably good investment. To keep that investment in good order will cost the owner quite a lot of money each year, although it should be worth it in the long run. Every house has its quirks, and the older the house the more quirks you find. Low ceilings and protruding beams that catch the unwary skull, wattle and daub walls that are far too thin to grant any degree of privacy, and appalling heating bills are just some of the incidental costs of living in an antique. Then there are the regular sums needed to keep thatched roofs in trim, maintain timber, repair plaster and brickwork, and keep the house painted. In return you get to live in a beautiful home, secure in the knowledge that you are helping to preserve a rare fragment of Britain's heritage.

But there is no shortage of Victorian houses – British cities are filled with row upon terraced row of them. And though they do indeed increase in value over time they are regarded by investor and home-owner alike as 'property' rather than 'antiques'. You buy Victorian because it is a house. Consequently, nineteenth-century property tends to be compared with modern houses, purpose-built for modern living, rather than with earlier dwellings. Owners who complain about thin walls, understructured roofs, shallow foundations, draughts and damp basements forget that these are exactly the sort of things an owner of an antique has to be prepared to live with and which a modern householder hopes to do without.

In general a Victorian house costs more to run than its modern equivalent. Apart from heating, the large, high-ceilinged rooms require more paint and paper than smaller modern rooms, and the often elaborate exterior timbers – bargeboards and the like – are expensive to maintain, usually requiring three storeys of scaffolding to reach them for painting. In return the old house offers more space than its post-war equivalent, with generous hallways, staircases and landings. Pound for pound, you get more house for your money if you buy Victorian. On the other hand, that house may prove expensive to insure,

Scaffolding is one of the major costs in maintaining or restoring a tall Victorian house.

because the cost of rebuilding it far outweighs the price you paid for it. But all in all a Victorian property is a very attractive item to would-be house buyers, though they have to be increasingly well-heeled as the price of such places rises. Estate agents who only a decade or so ago were extolling the virtues of completely modernized homes now talk pointedly of 'original features' and 'loving restoration'.

Original railings and tiles make all the difference at the entrance to an ordinary terraced house.

Certain agents specialize in old houses, although every agent has at least some Victorian property on its books – so much of it was built that it is hard to avoid. But on the whole the old property market tends to be rather amateurish, populated by owners without a clue about how to sell their historic house and developers and millionaires similarly uninformed on how to locate such buildings. The Department of the Environment used to fund a quarterly register of such buildings, but financial cuts have forced them to privatize the service and it is now run by the Historic Buildings Company. They offer a monthly catalogue called *The Period Property Register*, giving details of about four hundred old and historic houses ranging from Victorian to medieval, most of them a little on the expensive side.

The majority of purchasers of Victorian houses prefer to rely on their local estate agents, newspapers and their own nose. The middle range of property is unlikely to attract the specialist. Once you have found a house that you like, your problems start. The major building societies say that they do not make special rules for Victorian property and that they treat each mortgage prospect on its own merits. Whether you get a mortgage, and on what terms, will depend on your income, how much money you want, the state of the house you want to buy and the area in which the house is sited. Districts that suffer from declining house prices or subsidence can upset your building society.

An attractive frontage with all the right period details can often conceal expensive problems of restoration and maintenance.

Mass-produced mask keystones above the porches give these small terraced houses a sense of unity and elegance.

The nerve-racking and expensive business of buying a house – surveys, offers, conveyancing, stamp duty etc. – is fairly standard for any property. The Victorian house does, however, tend to offer certain 'original features' of which the house-hunter should be aware and which a survey will specifically examine. They can be briefly listed as roof, walls, timbers and foundations.

Understructured roofs are a common failing in Victorian houses. From the outside the roof may seem slightly bowed under the weight of the slates – possibly an indication that some work is needed on the roof. Missing slates may merely be the result of the last gale or could be the symptom of the charmingly named 'nail sickness' – effectively the nails that hold the slates to the battens may have become so corroded over the years that the slates start dropping off the roof. It can be expensive to replace those nails.

Houses for sale often boast freshly painted walls. It makes the interior seem fresh and attractive, but sometimes the paint also conceals cracks – often around door and window frames – that are a sign of movement in the walls and perhaps the foundations. The movement can be caused by anything from bulging walls, subsiding foundations and passing juggernauts to badly done plasterwork. A glance along the side of the outside walls, especially those that are not retained by joists – usually the side walls – may reveal a bulge in the wall. If this bulge is growing, the wall may need to be demolished and rebuilt; a minor bulge that in a surveyor's opinion has not moved for the last twenty years, on the other hand, may need no work at all. The usual compromise between neglect and total rebuilding is a tie bar, which stops any further movement. Newly painted walls can also conceal damp, which may be caused by exterior walls being constantly wetted by rainwater spilling from a damaged gutter, by condensation, or by true rising damp because of the failure or absence of a damp-proof course. The cure may be as simple as lowering a flowerbed or as extensive as replacing or installing an entire damp-proof course.

The timbers of windows and doors are easy to inspect despite recent repainting. If rotten they become very soft, as a little gentle prodding with a penknife will easily ascertain. Wet or dry rot in the main timbers of the house is harder to find, and less than scrupulous sellers have been known to recarpet a house to make it difficult to inspect under the floorboards. Despite the trouble, it is well worth unfixing and lifting some of the carpet so that you can take a look.

Unfortunately, you cannot get at foundations – the fourth category that needs checking. Faults with the foundations exhibit themselves through symptoms expressed in other parts of the house, such as rising damp because of DPC failure and deflection cracks caused by subsidence.

It is always advisable to pay for a survey by a trusted specialist; otherwise you may lose the house of your dreams to a bout of house-hunter's hypochondria, or find that it has become the house of your nightmares because of expensive and unforeseen problems. Although building societies nowadays let the buyer see the results of their own surveyor's inspection, these surveys are insufficiently detailed to be totally reliable.

Despite their hypochondria, once they have bought their Victorian house most owners expect a maintenance-free home when in fact they should anticipate having to spend steadily to keep the structure up to scratch. When money is tight, as it has been during the recession of the 1970s and 1980s, one of the first things people economize on is the more expensive items of

Gentrification in progress.

maintenance on their house. If a roof has lasted ninety or more winters, they feel, it can last another without harm. But the older that roof gets, the more fragile it becomes. When labour and materials were proportionally cheaper, roofs were maintained as a matter of course. Now, with a decent slate costing £2.50 (count how many £2.50s you have on your roof) there is a real incentive either just to patch up a roof or to postpone having the work done properly until you feel a bit richer. But a winter gale that merely dislodges a few slates can, in the end, do more damage that if it strips the roof bare. Because the slates are still on the roof – just a little out of position – there seems little need to worry. Some rain will start to seep in, but in such small amounts that it may never reach the ceiling; most of the water will be absorbed by the roof timbers themselves. Sooner or later the wet timbers, already overstressed, will start to rot. It is unlikely that anybody will notice: in most houses lofts are dark, rarely visited places. By the time the householder has got round to obtaining a quote for repairing the roof the job may have grown so dramatically that it may have to be postponed further until it can be afforded. Eventually the work will get done – maybe at the cost of this year's holiday or an extension of the mortgage. If the money cannot be found then the roof could remain neglected until one day the hapless householder finds an open-air loft.

It is rather like ignoring the oil warning light in car until the car suddenly grinds to a smelly and smoking halt with a ruined engine. It leaves an angry and out-of-pocket car-owner but the damaged car deprives nobody else. A house that is damaged beyond repair by neglect, however, may cost the current householder dear but it also deprives future generations. The few good houses from the fourteenth century that survive by a combination of luck and careful management have been homes to numerous generations. If a Victorian house is to last another five centuries – which it may well do, being usually better built than a fourteenth-century cottage – then by allowing it to slide into disrepair you may also be putting countless future generations out on the street. In the long term, therefore, the community gains more from keeping a house in good repair than does the current householder, so in certain cases the community bears some of the cost of those repairs.

In England and Wales around half of all houses were built before 1940, and a third before 1919. The majority of those pre-1919 houses are the result of the huge nineteenth-century boom in house-building. The English and Welsh House Condition Surveys of 1981 found that nearly one-quarter of the housing stock was unsatisfactory in some way. More houses had basic amenities like bathrooms and toilets than at the time of the last survey, in 1976, but this was outweighed by a rise in the number of homes needing major repairs. Nearly

Polychromatic brickwork and bargeboarding – an interesting example of late Victorian Gothic that is well worth preserving.

four million homes, the survey reported, needed repairs costing over £2500, and these problem homes were concentrated in the older stock and in the owner-occupied sector. In short, as the housing stock gets older and Britain gets poorer, so more and more Victorian houses are being allowed to subside into decay. Those houses are not being replaced by modern building either: since 1979, according to a statement made by Shelter in 1986, public money being invested in housing has been cut by 40 per cent, despite the fact that official figures for the rate of household formation show a need for a minimum building programme of 200,000 homes a year. So old houses are not only disappearing faster than they are being replaced, but are doing so at a time when homelessness is increasing.

At this point the logical step is the application of government money, in the form of grants, to enable householders of older properties to improve the condition of their houses and thus to increase the housing stock. Indeed for a number of years this was true, with the government making substantial funds available first for pre-1919 property, and then extending it to cover pre-1939 property. But so many people took advantage of these grants that inevitably funds dwindled. Grant money has always been administered by local councils, and was therefore subject to the policies of these authorities. Labour-run councils, for instance, were often unwilling to give large grants to owner-occupiers because 'gentrification' of an area might completely change its social and therefore its political character; they also preferred to direct their money towards public-sector housing. However, at the time of writing all councils, whatever their political colour, have had to cut back, and there is no guarantee that you will receive any but mandatory grants. Details of all the possible grants and some of the conditions attached to them are given below; but do keep in touch with your local council, too, because central and local government policies are constantly changing.

There are basically three kinds of grant, called intermediate grants, improvement grants and repair grants. They should be regarded only as contributions towards the cost of the work – the council never pays the whole amount. Intermediate grants are mandatory – the council is obliged to give them to all applicants; improvement grants and repair grants are discretionary – so you may or may not get your money (and you will not get an improvement grant if the rateable value of your house is more than £400 in Greater London or £225 elsewhere). All of these grants are available to owner-occupiers, but the situation is more complex for tenants and cannot adequately be explained here; ask your council for information and advice. It is important to apply for any grant, and receive the council's approval in writing, *before* you start doing any relevant work on the house; otherwise you may find yourself in the position of getting no grant at all.

Intermediate grants enable you to put into your property basic amenities that it lacks: these are an inside lavatory, sink, washbasin, bath, and hot and cold water. Improvement grants are for major improvements to houses in very poor condition. Repair grants are for major repairs on pre-1919 houses in which you are not also undertaking improvements. The likelihood of your getting either of the two types of discretionary grant, the amount of the grant, and the kind of work that you are allowed to have done on your house may all depend on whether you live in certain officially designated categories of property or area, described below. The Planning Department of your local council will tell you if any of them applies to your house.

Below left: Stone-effect cladding is often applied out of well-meant ignorance.

Below: One solution to the problems of bringing decaying old property up to modern building standards is to demolish and rebuild in a style that matches the remainder of the terrace. Infill buildings are becoming more common – and if done well often go unnoticed.

A building can, for instance, be 'listed' because it is of 'architectural or historic interest' – though this is unlikely to happen to run-of-the-mill Victorian town houses. Special consent is required before certain types of change can be made to the interior or exterior of a listed property. But beware: if you are offered a grant for work on a listed building the council may insist on other work also being done that you had not budgeted for; or it may demand that the work is carried out to modern specifications that conflict with the basic nature (and *raison d'être* for listing) of your period house! An alternative to listing a particular building or street is for the council to apply what is known as an Article 4 to specific parts of a house or street. It can be used to prevent the removal of trees from a street or to stop the erosion of front gardens by concreting them to make parking spaces. The most common control imposed by councils, however, is the establishment of Conservation Areas – a way of loosely listing an area worth preserving which is often applied to streets or suburbs of Victorian houses. It gives councils surprisingly little power beyond having a say in whether or not you may demolish your house, but it can be combined with or strengthened by an Article 4 on the specific features that are seen as important.

On a wider front there are Housing Action Areas, Enveloping Schemes and General Improvement Areas. Housing Action Areas indicate council concern for local housing to be improved. If you live in a HAA you may find it easier to get housing grants, and the grants you get will be bigger – sometimes as high as 95 per cent of the cost of the work. In return, within HAAs compulsory purchase is easier for councils, who can buy up a house they think is being left to fall into decay. Housing Action Areas are unusual in that, under certain conditions, money can be granted to tenants – rather than owner-occupiers – for basic improvements. Enveloping Schemes are supposed to make an area more desirable. The council renovates the exteriors of houses in the hope that it will encourage householders to stay in the area, improve the interiors of their houses and attract more people to move into the area. General Improvement Areas take this cosmetic approach a stage further, combining Envelopment with Housing Action. Improvement grant availability is increased while the council concentrates on doing up the streets and exteriors of the area.

Inevitably there are disagreements over the utility and effectiveness of these ways of implementing housing policies. Local councils are administering government money and they have to show that they are doing this properly – but showing often gets in the way of doing. As one planning officer put it: 'The biggest vandals in the borough are the council themselves.' Housing associations are a good example. Exemplary bodies whose main aim is to make living space for as many people as economically as possible, they naturally take as much advantage as possible of any money on offer. A lot of the property that they restore is Victorian, and often very run down. To obtain the grants it needs a housing association has to restore the property to modern (not Victorian) standards of structural integrity. Any structure of two storeys and above requires a lot of work to conform with modern standards. That work can cost a housing association £50,000 per house before it has even started making any modifications to the living space. In addition, the council is forced to demand that the building be guaranteed for thirty to fifty years by the architect and builder responsible. The house must therefore have all its old timbers either stripped out and replaced, or radically fire- and insect-proofed, and the result is a structure that has been gutted and rebuilt at great expense – the majority of the grant has been spent on vandalizing a house rather than making it habitable.

Whether or not you get a grant, the questions of Planning Permission and Building Regulations have to be considered. Some people, fearful of becoming submerged in planning bureaucracy, prefer to employ builders direct without using an architect as a middleman. It is a quirk of legislation that architects have to inform the council of planned changes to a structure; builders are not legally obliged to do so, and often don't. But by avoiding the bureaucracy you may also be depriving yourself of a great deal of free and useful advice. Not only will the conservation or planning officer be able to give you an idea of what may best suit your house, but he or she may also be able to put you in touch with specialist architects, builders and tradesmen as well as useful sources of background information like a local history society or archive. And on a practical note the council can make you demolish any building work of which you have not informed them and which does not conform to the regulations.

Planning Permission is in general concerned with protecting the appearance of a street or locality, and by extension the interests of its residents; it is the refusal of Planning Permission that will prevent, for instance, a smelly factory being sited in a vacant space in your residential street, or your neighbour from putting up a garage that cuts out the daylight from your kitchen. Building Regulations, on the other hand, are concerned with quality of work; the council will want to be satisfied, for instance, that the foundations of your planned new extension will be structurally sound. So despite the irksome form-filling, and the waiting, these systems may well save you from eyesores and cowboy builders. Approval of Planning Permission is often affected by whether you live in any of the special categories described above (for example a listed building or a Conservation Area). Many people confuse Planning Permission with Building

Architectural salvage yards are treasure houses for those who want to restore original features to their house, or build a sympathetic extension.

Regulations, or regard the latter as part of the former. They are separate entities, and you may well find yourself needing to apply for Building Regulations approval but not for Planning Permission. Full details can be obtained from the Planning Department of your local council. As with grants, the appropriate application should be made, and approval received in writing, before you start the work.

For a time it was fashionable to describe houses as machines for living. As a machine, the Victorian house is flexible, practical and durable: it does not suffer from built-in obsolescence; on the other hand it has been superseded by modern models boasting superior features. The Victorian house has solid walls that let in the cold and sometimes the damp; it is usually draughty; and it often has very shallow foundations.

But to call a house a machine is to ignore a part of it. All houses have a personality of a sort – sometimes it is merely a reflection of the owner's personality, but, if you are lucky, the house may have a unity that gives it its own personality. The look and feel of the house, its advantages and imperfections all contribute to the way we – as either owner or visitor – regard the place. But one can go too far in building up this cult of the personality, and end up unable to carry out even the slightest degree of modernization in case the house's integrity is damaged. The sensible way is a balance of the two, and it depends on knowledge. It is rarely philistine zeal that compels a house-owner to cover a property in limestone cladding; it is often ignorance. Why else would somebody spend £2000 on cladding that will reduce the value of the house and may damage the original fabric of the building? Those monstrosities that the experts keep pointing out in the middle of carefully preserved terraces are not usually constructed out of a hatred for the original building; they are the work of a sensible householder who wants a dry roof and windows that do their job.

The problem is how to avoid making similar mistakes. Every terrace is slightly different from the next, and the distinction between styles of houses built in different parts of the country or in different decades of the nineteenth century can be quite dramatic. Even within the ambit of a single local council there will often be sufficient variety in Victorian houses to make it impossible for a conservation officer to tell you exactly the kinds of things that are best for your particular house. You are going to have to do a little homework if you want to find out the right kind of sash window, the style of railings and the kinds of cornices your house had originally. You can, of course, call in experts who specialize in house restoration. But experts cost money. It can be cheaper and more fun to do most of the groundwork yourself, saving your money for the work that really needs specialist skills.

7. History of Your House

Where you begin depends on what you want to know. If you just need to find the pattern of the shutters that the previous owner of your house removed, so that you can replace them, the answer is often simple. Take a look at your neighbour's house; the chances are that the particular item you are interested in has survived in at least one house in the road. Failing that, you will need to find some old photographs or plans of the house – and in the process of tracking them down you might also discover when the house was built, the names of some of the people who lived in it, and a little of the history of your area. The place to start with all these questions is your local history library.

Every region of Britain has an archive of local history material, usually divided between particular libraries (local history libraries) and record offices. There should be one of each covering your city, town or county. If in doubt, ask at your local public library. A local record office may be relatively intimidating to approach; it would be wise to write or telephone in advance, making an appointment to see some specific material. A local history library will probably have a more informal approach and be able to advise you on how to go about your search, so start there.

Since London is not only well supplied with records but also convenient, let us take as an example a medium-sized house in Clerkenwell. In 1986 it has four bedrooms, a front and back parlour, a basement kitchen and all the usual mod cons. The title deeds show that it was built in 1843. If the deeds had been destroyed or were not easily accessible, there would have been other ways of finding out when the house was built.

Start with the nineteenth-century equivalent of the telephone directory. These trade directories began in London in the seventeenth century and by the eighteenth century had reached most provincial cities and towns. They are still published, and the best-known one is Kelly's. The earliest directories list houses alphabetically by the names of their owners. Clerkenwell had a lot of clockmakers until the 1820s, so if the Clerkenwell house were built early enough it might well be listed under, say, 'Mr Jones, Clockmaker', followed by the address. It can be a bit of a slog running down column after column looking

Left above: A tea party in a garden, *c.* 1865.

Left below: A family group taken at a christening.

Below: Three turn-of-the-century children.

for the address. On the other hand, there were a lot fewer people a century or so back, so the task is simpler than you might at first imagine.

Happily, the directories began listing houses by street after about 1817, which makes life much easier. By simply checking through each year's directory you should eventually reach the earliest listing for that address. The Clerkenwell house is in Cumberland Gardens, and the first entry for that street is 1843. This confirms the date on the title deeds. It also names the owner: René Dubois, Diamond Merchant. The French name is probably of Huguenot origin and Clerkenwell was a favoured area for these Protestant refugees. Clerkenwell is a short walk away from Hatton Garden, then and now a thriving market in precious stones. A quick cross-check with the trade section shows that M. Dubois had his own precious stone business in Hatton Garden.

Census returns are also useful. Censuses have been carried out every ten years in Britain since 1801, but the reports are only released a century later, to protect people's privacy. Census reports are available at the Census Office in Kingsway, London, but most local history libraries keep on microfiche copies of the reports for their own areas, and the librarian will be able either to let you have a look at them or to tell where they are stored. Initially the census was simply a head count of the parish population, houses and families, with some occupational information. The General Register Office, established in 1837, managed a more sophisticated census in 1841 which listed the name, occupation, address, approximate age and origins of each person. The 1851 census was more refined, detailing marital status, relationship to the head of the household, exact age, parish and county of birth. Returns for 1841, 1851, 1861, 1871 and 1881 have been collected in five books. Enumerators' books, which contain the raw data on which the census was based, are often also kept on microfiche by local libraries.

This photograph by Paul Martin of children dancing to an organ grinder also provides a lot of information about the terrace in the background.

A street market, photographed by Paul Martin.

From the enumerator's book for Clerkenwell it seems that René Dubois lived with his wife, a maiden aunt, five children and two live-in servants. (Incidentally, it is sometimes easy to confuse the enumerator's number for the household with the house number. 'No. 7 Cumberland Gardens' may refer to the seventh household visited, rather than the postal address.) A late census reveals that the Clerkenwell house was inhabited by a widow and her son. Her son is listed as an art student attending the Royal Academy. A check with the Royal Academy archives shows that he was indeed a student, a very promising young artist who died at the tragically early age of twenty-eight before his career had been properly established. The current owner of the Clerkenwell house was even able to trace and buy some of the young man's paintings.

But before getting side-tracked into other archives it is worth noting that ratebooks, one of the least-used records, can fill in an astonishing amount of detail only hinted at by the census. A check of the valuation rolls held in Perth archives in Scotland (which only date back to 1860) on Cleeve House, a

RUISLIP STREET

property of similar vintage to the Clerkenwell one revealed that it used to be called Oakbent House and was part of a larger estate that has now been built over. The owner of the estate, Francis Norrie Miller, lived in the house and was head of the General Accident Company and Provost of Perth. The house now looks across the valley to the new high-tech headquarters of General Accident. Valuation rolls (which were updated annually) or ratebooks should give the municipal valuation of the house and the names and occupations of the owner and tenant. It will also reveal what the house consisted of in that year. An early ratebook describes the Clerkenwell house as a 'dwelling house and yard twenty square feet. Two workshops'; it was early enough in the century to work from home without loss of face.

History in the making. The Prince and Princess of Wales, later King George V and Queen Mary, opening the Totterdown Estate in Tooting, South London, in 1903.

Depending on where you live, other information may be available to help you in your search. In London and other large cities and towns, for example, sewer records can provide a useful check on the date of your house. After about 1860, the first thing you did when you moved into a new house was have it connected to the sewers. The sewer record therefore gives not only the year in which the house was built, but probably the exact date when it was first occupied. Locating sewer records is a little difficult following the abolition of metropolitan councils like the GLC. Who inherits their archives is still in some doubt at the time of writing, but as a consolation many an enterprising local archive has copies of such material. As always, start with your local history library.

The rich and the well-to-do tend to be carefully documented. They paid taxes, voted, owned property, attended social events that got reported in the papers, and so on. Local newspapers may seem like a good source of background to the researcher, but they tend to be too much of a good thing. The headlines and photographs that leaven modern newspapers are absent, and it can be a drudge to plough through an old paper. It is better to ask for guidance from the librarian, who may know of specialist cuttings files or of some cataloguing that may have been done. The poor, without property, are harder to track down – unless they had a criminal record sufficient to be noted at quarter sessions. These are reasonably complete from 1800 onwards, and are located in the Public Record Office in England and the National Library in Wales. They are useful for following the careers of black sheep in the family, but little help in establishing the history of a house.

The Tithe Commutation Act of 1836 set out to tidy up the ragbag system of paying for the support of the parish parson. To do this, liabilities had to be mapped out and written down, providing valuable evidence of the existence of people and property. Tithe maps for your parish can be complex and confusing things to deal with, and it may well be worth consulting a more expert book on the subject before you start. The maps can be obtained either from the National Library in Wales, who have excellent map-copying facilities, or from the Public Record Office in England, who are not cheap. In addition some local history libraries have the ones for their area.

The Ordnance Survey was established at the end of the eighteenth century to map the maritime counties of southern England in preparation for a possible French invasion. The work was slowly extended until by 1870 a continuous set of one-inch-to-the-mile maps of the whole country had been completed – most of which were out of date. The expansion of the railways and the cities changed the face of England faster than it could be mapped. For this and other reasons, the dates on maps do not necessarily mean that what is on the map actually

existed; some maps, for example, show proposed railways that were never built. But, as the quick look at Stoke Newington High Street in Chapter 4 showed, OS maps can be a very useful supplement to other sources.

Each library and archive has its own unique sources – sometimes an unpublished local history, the archive of a local business, photograph albums and even inventories and wills. Digging through them may mean winnowing an awful lot of chaff; but it is often very interesting chaff, and the odd grain you discover may be just the one that will grow and fruit in the way you want. The particularly saintly researcher might also catalogue these archives as he or she goes, or at least leave notes on them for those that come after.

These various ways of finding out about the history of your house neglect the history that your house can tell you; a little knowledge of architecture and building techniques can reveal more about your house than do the title deeds. In the 1950s, at Manchester University, this was formalized into a systematic procedure for studying vernacular architecture. The various parts of a building, what they are made of, how they are placed in position to each other and how the building stands in relation to other buildings are combined to give a rapid but detailed summary of local styles and materials. This system, which is unlikely to appeal to you unless your interest already has a professional edge, is fully explained in R.W. Brunskill's *Illustrated Handbook of Vernacular Architecture* (1970) and neatly summarized in Philip Riden's *Local History – A Handbook for Beginners* (1983). Using the Manchester system it is possible to tell a great deal about a house just by looking at it, provided you know what you are looking for.

Most books on tracing the history of your home, including Riden's *Local History*, assume you want to go back more than a century. Since Victorian houses are only a century or so old, their origins are more accessible, and there are still a few people alive who recall the construction of Victorian suburbs in the 1890s. But beware oral history. In her history of Kentish Town, *The Fields Beneath*, Gillian Tindall writes that

Left above: Modest terraced houses and shops, *c.* 1889.

Left: The Victorians invented the public park, without which no suburb was complete.

talking to old people in the course of compiling this book, I was again and again told 'Cows were grazed at Gospel Oak when I was a girl', or 'It used to be all fields around here, dear; I remember before such-and-such a street was built.' Reference to a map of the period shows this not in fact to have been the case. Every street in central Kentish Town was there before the birth of the oldest person now living – indeed large parts of the district are now so old that they have reached the rebuilding stage; the crop of houses has been sown anew. What appears to be significant about these 'reminiscences' (which are regularly reproduced by gullible local newspaper editors) is not their objective truth but the fact that people of all ages *wish* to believe they are true.

The 'grazing cows' turn out to be animals unloaded from the railway yards being driven to the slaughterhouse. To this day there are meat-processing factories in Kentish Town.

One of the attractions of the past is its romance; one of the fascinations of that past is the elusive mixture of the mundane and the ridiculous that brings history to life. The owner of Oakbank House, on the outskirts of Perth, investigated what local opinion held to be the ruins of a big house that must once have dominated the village of Cherrybank. Cherrybank has now been absorbed into the town of Perth, and there was little left of the house beyond an imposing gatepost and extensive overgrown foundations that ran down to the edge of the burn that still runs through the valley into the River Tay. A little research at the local library soon turned up the true origins of this mysterious ruin: Second World War piggeries.

An itinerant cutler sharpening knives in the street, photographed by Paul Martin.

FURTHER READING

There are two main specialist magazines, *Traditional Homes* and *Period Homes*, that come out each month. *Traditional Homes* was the most useful and practical in our experience, not least because its publisher, C F E Publishing Ltd, also produces a quarterly *Traditional Interior Decoration* and *Traditional Kitchens*, and the annuals *Traditional Homes Book of Heating, Plumbing and Bathrooms, Traditional Home Repairs* and *Traditional Homes Trade and Services Directory. See* Useful Addresses.

British Leisure Publications produce a helpful annual guide called *Museums and Galleries of Great Britain and Ireland,* which they say is a comprehensive guide to over 1100 museums and art galleries, indexed by area and subject. Each museum gets a brief description accompanied by its address, opening times and facilities. *See* Useful Addresses.

The National Trust publish a similar annual directory of their properties for members and visitors. *See* Useful Addresses.

Although a little too expensive for most readers to consider purchasing, *A Pictorial Dictionary of Nineteenth Century Furniture Design* (Antique Collectors Club, 1977), is a good starting place for researching furniture dates and styles. Your local reference library may have a copy.

What follows is a selection of books that may inform or entertain:

Putting Back the Style: A Directory of Authentic Renovation, edited by Alexandra Artley,
    Evans, 1982
The New Georgian Handbook, Alexandra Artley and John Martin Robinson,
    Ebury Press, 1985
The National Trust Book of the English House, Aslet and Powers, Viking, 1985
Victorian Cities, Asa Briggs, Pelican, 1968
A Social History of Housing, John Burnett, David and Charles, 1978
The Victorian Underworld, Kellow Chesney, Pelican, 1972
The Opulent Eye, Nicholas Cooper, Architectural Press, 1976
The Victorian Garden, Tom Carter, Bell and Hyman, 1984
The Butler's Pantry Book, Elizabeth Drury, A. and C. Black, 1981

Victorian Suburb: A Study of the Growth of Camberwell, H. J. Dyos,
    Leicester University Press, 1961

Sweetness and Light, Mark Girouard, Yale University Press, 1984

The Diary of a Nobody, George and Weedon Grossmith, Penguin Modern Classics, 1965

How to Restore and Improve Your Victorian House, The Hackney Society

From Tower to Tower Block, The Hackney Society

Victorian England as Seen by Punch, Frank E. Huggett, Sidgwick and Jackson, 1978

Paint Magic, Jocasta Innes, Windward/Berger Paints, 1981

Discovering Your Old House, David Iredale, Shire Publications, 1968

How to Restore and Improve Your Victorian House, Alan Johnson,
    David and Charles, 1984

Vanishing Victoriana, Lucinda Lambton, Elsevier Phaidon, 1976

Temples of Convenience, Lucinda Lambton, Gordon Fraser, 1978

The English Terraced House, Stefan Muthesius, Yale University Press, 1982

Local History: A Handbook for Beginners, Philip Riden, Batsford, 1983

The Fields Beneath, Gillian Tindall, Granada, 1980

The Making of the Industrial Landscape, Barrie Trinder, Dent, 1982

The History of Gardens, Christopher Thacker, Croom Helm, 1979

The Making of Modern London 1815–1914, Gavin Weightman and Steve Humphries,
    Sidgwick and Jackson, 1983

Rats, Lice and History: the Biography of a Bacillus, Hans Zinsser, Papermac, 1985

USEFUL ADDRESSES

In the process of researching the television series and writing this book we made contact with a number of organizations whose names and addresses may be useful. Although idiosyncratic and selective, this list may help point you in the right direction. Museums are given in a separate list on p.170.

Apsley House
Hyde Park Corner,
London W1
Tel: 01 499 5676
 See **Museums**

Architectural Heritage Fund
Civic Trust
17 Carlton House Terrace
London SW1Y 5AW
Tel: 01 930 0914
 Low-interest loans to amenity groups restoring old buildings

Architectural Heritage Society of
Scotland, 5b Forres Street
Edinburgh
Tel: 031 225 9724
 Formerly Scottish Georgian Society

Association for Industrial Archaeology
The Wharfage, Ironbridge
Telford, Shropshire
Tel: 0952 453522

Bath Preservation Trust
1 Royal Crescent, Bath, Somerset
Tel: 0225 27229

Bath Society, 14 Queen Square
Bath, Somerset
Tel: 0225 29770
 Split from Bath Preservation Trust in 1970s

Brick Development Association
Woodside House, Winkfield
Windsor, Berks
Tel: 0344 885651
 Advice on brick problems

British Architectural Library and Drawings
Collection
66 Portland Place, London W1 (*library*)
and
21 Portman Square
London W1 (*drawings*)
Tel: 01 580 5533
 Foremost architectural library in Britain

British Historic Buildings Trust
68 Battersea High Street
London SW11
Tel: 01 228 3336

British Leisure Publications
Windsor Court, East Grinstead House
East Grinstead, West Sussex
RH19 1XA
Tel: 0342 26972
 Publish 'Museums and Galleries in Great Britain and Ireland' (*see* Further Reading)

British Wood Preservation Association
Premier House, 150 Southampton Row
London WC1
Tel: 01 837 8217
 Advice on wood

Brooking Collection
Woodhay, White Lane
Guildford, Surrey
Tel: 0483 504 555
   See **Museums**

Building Centre, 26 Store Street
London WC1
Tel: 01 637 1022
Enquiry service 0344 884999
Computer centre 01-636 0512
Brick advisory service 01 637 0047
   To colour-match bricks
Bookshop 01 637 3151

Building Conservation Trust
Apartment 39, Hampton Court Palace
East Molesey, Surrey KT8 9BS
Tel: 01 943 2277
   Advice and information.
   See also **Museums**

CFE Publishing Ltd, Scharpps House
Grosvenor Road, St Albans
Herts AL1 3AD
Tel: 0727 59166
   Publish 'Traditional Homes'
   magazine etc.

Charles Rennie Mackintosh Society
Queens Cross, 870 Garscube Road
Glasgow
Tel: 041 646 6600

Chartered Institute of Building Services
Delta House, 22 Balham High Road
London SW12
Tel: 01 675 5211
   Advice on plumbing, heating and
   ventilation in old houses

Civic Trust, 17 Carlton House Terrace
London SW1Y 5AW
Tel: 01 930 0614
   General advice on environmental
   problems

Civic Trust for Scotland
24 George Square, Glasgow
Tel: 041 221 1466
   General advice on environmental
   problems

Civic Trust for Wales (Treftadaeth Cymru)
St Michael's College, Llandaff
Cardiff
Tel: 0222 552388
   General advice on environmental
   problems

Conservation Bureau, Rosebery House
Haymarket Terrace, Edinburgh
Tel: 031 337 9595
   Register of conservation
   craftsmen

Construction History Society
c/o Chartered Institute of Building
Englemere, Kings Ride
Ascot, Berks SL5 8BJ
Tel: 0990 23355

Crafts Council, 12 Waterloo Place
London SW1Y 4AY
Tel: 01 930 4811

Decorative Arts Society
c/o Brighton Museum, Brighton
East Sussex
Tel: 0273 603005

English Heritage
   See **Historic Buildings and**
   Monuments Commission

English Tourist Board
4 Grosvenor Gardens, London SW1
Tel: 01 730 3488

Federation of Master Builders
33 John Street, London WC1
Tel: 01 242 7583

Furniture History Society
c/o Department of Furniture
Victoria and Albert Museum
Exhibition Road, London SW7
Tel: 01 589 6371

Garden History Society
66 Granville Park, London SE13
Tel: 01 852 1818
   Publishes journal 'Garden
   History'

Georgian Society, 37 Spital Square
London E1 6DY
Tel: 01 377 1722

Historic Buildings Company
Chobham Park House, Chobham, Surrey
Tel: 09905 7983/7196
   **Publish 'The Period Property
   Register' of listed houses for sale**

Historic Buildings and Monuments
Commission
Fortress House, 23 Savile Row
London W1X 1AB
Tel: 01 734 6010
   **Also known as English
   Heritage. Conservation
   organization**

Institute for Industrial Archaeology
Ironbridge Gorge Museum, Ironbridge
Telford, Shropshire TF8 7AW
Tel: 095 245 3522

Institute of Plumbers
Scottish Mutual House, North Street
Hornchurch, Essex RM11 1RU
Tel: 040 24 45199

Landmark Trust, 21 Deans Yard
London SW1
Tel: 01 222 6581
   **Publishes 'Landmark Handbook'
   of eccentric buildings to let**

London Stained Glass Repository
Glaziers Hall, 9 Montague Close
London SE1 9DD
Tel: 01 403 3300 and 01 407 1109

Men of the Stones, The Rutlands
Stamford, Lincs
Tel: 0780 63372
   Advice on stonemasonry

National Trust, 42 Queen Anne's Gate
London SW1
Tel: 01 222 9251

National Trust for Scotland
5 Charlotte Square, Edinburgh
Tel: 031 226 5922

Paint Research Association
Waldegrave Road, Teddington, Middx
Tel: 01 977 4427
   Advice on paint

Royal Horticulural Society
Horticultural Hall, Vincent Square
London SW1
Tel: 01 834 4333

Royal Institute of British Architects
66 Portland Place, London W1
Tel: 01 580 5533

Save Britain's Heritage
68 Battersea High Street
London SW11
Tel: 01 228 3336

Society of Architectural Historians of
Great Britain
Room 208, Chesham House
30 Warwick Street, London W1
Tel: 01 734 8144 Ext. 13

Society for the Protection of Ancient
Buildings
37 Spital Square, London E1 6DY
Tel: 01 377 1644

Spitalfields Trust
19 Princelet Street, London E1
Tel: 01 247 0971

Town and Country Planning Association
17 Carlton House Terrace
London SW1
Tel: 01 930 8903
   Advice on planning

Victorian Society, 1 Priory Gardens
London W4
Tel: 01 994 1019
   **Among other activities, runs
   Linley Sambourne House**

William Morris Society
26 Upper Mall, London W6
Tel: 01 748 5618

MUSEUMS

Abbeydale Industrial Hamlet
Abbeydale Road South, Sheffield S7 2QW
Tel: 0742 367731
Working industrial machinery

Apsley House (Wellington Museum)
Hyde Park Corner, London W1
Tel: 01 499 5676
Trophies, uniforms and paintings

Avery Historical Museum
W. & T. Avery Ltd, Foundry Lane
Warley, West Midlands B66 2LP
Tel: 021 558 1112
Weighing machines

Avoncroft Museum of Building
Stoke Prior, Bromsgrove, Hereford
and Worcester B60 4JR
Tel: 0527 31363
Operational windmill, eighteenth-century earth closet, etc.

Beamish North of England Open Air
Museum
Beamish, near Stanley, Co. Durham
DH9 0RG
Tel: 0207 231811
Co-op shops, Victorian pubs, colliery, pit cottages, farm and locomotives in steam

Black Country Museum, Tipton Road
Dudley, West Midlands DY1 4SQ
Tel: 021 557 9643
Shops, pub, canal, cottages, coalmine, trams, beam engine, chainmaking and glass-cutting

British Engineerium, Nevill Road
Hove, East Sussex BN3 7QA
Tel: 0273 559583
Working steam engines of all sizes

British Museum
Great Russell Street, London WC1
Tel: 01 636 1555

Brooking Collection, Woodhay
White Lane, Guildford, Surrey
Tel: 0483 504 555
Windows and architectural furnishings, by appointment only

Building Conservation Trust
Apartment 39, Hampton Court Palace
East Molesey, Surrey KT8 9BS
Tel: 01 943 2277
'Care of Buildings' exhibition on maintenance problems

Chiltern Open Air Museum
Newland Park, Chalfont St Giles
Bucks
Tel: 024 07 71117
Farm buildings and tollhouse

Dickens House Museum
48 Doughty Street, London WC2
Tel: 01 405 2127

Geffrye Museum, Kingsland Road
London E2 8EA
Tel: 01 739 8368/9893
Period rooms from 1600 to 1939

Gladstone Pottery Museum
26 Uttoxeter Road, Longton
Stoke-on-Trent ST3 1PQ
Tel: 0782 311378

Great Western Railway Museum
Faringdon Road, Swindon, Wilts
Tel: 0793 26161

Grosvenor Museum
27 Grosvenor Street, Chester CH1 2DD
Tel: 0244 21616/313858
Reconstructed nineteenth-century pub interior

Institute of Agricultural History and
Museum of English Rural Life
Reading University, Whiteknights
PO Box 229, Reading, Berks RG6 2AG
Tel: 0734 875123
History of English countryside

Ironbridge Gorge Museum
Ironbridge, Telford, Shropshire TF8 7AW
Tel: 095 245 2751
**World's first iron bridge, museum
of iron, Coalport China Museum,
Jackfield Tile Museum, Bliss Hill
industrial community (1905) and
Rosehill House – home of Darby
family of ironmasters**

Linley Sambourne House
18 Stafford Terrace, London W8
Tel: 01 994 1019
**Late nineteenth-century 'artistic'
house carefully preserved by
Victorian Society**

London Transport Museum
39 Wellington Street, London WC2
Tel: 01 379 6344
**Horse and motor buses, trolley
buses, trams and underground
rolling stock**

Museum of Childhood
Cambridge Heath Road
Bethnal Green, London E2
Tel: 01 980 2415

Museum of Chimney Pots
8 Percy Gardens, Blandford, Dorset
Tel: 0258 52290
**By appointment with the
Rev. Valentine Fletcher**

Museum of Labour History
Limehouse Town Hall
Commercial Road, London E14
Tel: 01 515 3229

Museum of London, 150 London Wall
London EC2
Tel: 01 600 3699
**Nineteenth-century shop and
room reconstructions**

National Portrait Gallery
2 St Martin's Place, London WC2
Tel: 01 930 1552

National Railway Museum
Leeman Road, York YO2 4XJ
Tel: 0904 21261

Science Museum
Exhibition Road, London SW7
Tel: 01 589 3456

Silver Studio Collection
Middlesex Polytechnic
Bounds Green Road, London N11 2NQ
Tel: 01 368 1299
**Designs and samples of fabric and
wallpaper from nineteenth-
century studio**

Sir John Soane's Museum
13 Lincoln's Inn Fields
London WC2A 3BP
Tel: 01 405 2107
Odd mix of antiquities and art

Steamtown, Carnforth, Cumbria
Tel: 052 473 4220/2100

Victoria and Albert Museum
Exhibition Road, London SW7
Tel: 01 589 6371
Kershaw's panels and a lot more

Weald and Downland Open Air Museum
Singleton, Chichester, West Sussex
Tel: 024 363 348
**Rescued historic buildings from
medieval times onwards**

INDEX

Page numbers in *italic* refer to the illustrations

Abbey Place Studios, St John's Wood, *30*
air pollution, 136
Albert, Prince Consort, 80
alcohol, 100–2, 109
apprenticeships, 35
Apsley House, London, 92, 94
architects, 28, 35, 70–2, 152
architectural salvage, 124, *153*
archives, 155–63
Article 4, 151
Artley, Alexandra, 120
Arts and Crafts movement, 91, 117–18
attics, 50

back extensions, 82, 137, 138
back-to-back housing, 28, 43
balusters, 55
bargeboards, *148*
basements, 37, 134–5
Bath, 76, 95
bathrooms, 82–4, *83–5*, 135–6, *135*
bathtubs, 82–3
Bazalgette, Sir Joseph, 80
Beaufort Pedestal Closet, 80–1, *81*
bedrooms, 58–9, 76
Beeton, Mrs, 110–11, 123, 129–30, 132
Bermondsey, 12
Besant, Sir Walter, 105
Bethnal Green, *22*
Birkenhead Park, Liverpool, 109
Birmingham, 40
Bissell, 134
Booth's Trolley-Vac, *133*
breakfast rooms, 62
bricklayers, 35
bricks and brickwork, *44*
    bonds, 41–2
    brickmaking, 26
    extensions, 138
    foundations, 37–8
    mortar, 40–1
    party walls, 43
    polychromatic, *33, 40*, 41, *148*
    secondhand, 42
    stucco, 45–7
    types, 41
bronze, 94

Brooking, Charles, 53
Brooking Collection, 52, 53
Brown, Capability, 113
Brunskill, R.W., 163
Budding, Edwin Beard, 114
The Builder, 82, 102, 109
builders, 152
    speculative builders, 22–3, 28, 31, 35–6
The Building News, 30
Building Regulations, 137–8, 152–4
Building Research Establishment, 136–7
building societies, 143, 145
Burdett-Coutts, Angela, 24, *108*
Burgess Park, Camberwell, 35
buses, 17
butlers, 130
buying Victorian houses, 140–54
'by-law' houses, 29–31
by-laws, 29–31

Camberwell, 35
Camden Town, *12*
Carey, Robert, 98–100
carpets, 75
cast iron, *92*
catalogues, shop, 76
cavity walls, 41, 138
ceiling heights, 137–8
ceiling roses, 89
cellars, 36–7, 78
cemeteries, 105–6, *106, 107*, 110
Census Office, 158
censuses, 158–9
central heating, 86, *86*, 125
Central Park, New York, 109
cess pits, 80
Cherrybank, Perth, 164
Chesney, Kellow, 15, 98
child mortality, 105, 132
children, 132
cholera, 83
churches, 101
City of London, 11, 12, 14
cladding, stone-effect, *150*, 154
classicism, 93–4
clay subsoils, 38
Clean Air Act, 120
cleaning, 25–6, 59–60, 130–2
Cleeve House, Perth, 159–60

Clerkenwell, 155–60
coal fires, 86–7, 120, 124
colour, interior decoration, 63, 65–7
Compton Hall, Wolverhampton, *129*
compulsory purchase, 151
concrete tiles, 47
condensation, 136, 145
Conservation Areas, 151, 152
conservatories, *111, 112, 115*, 116
Cooper, Nicholas, 63, 127
County Hall, London, 100
couple close roofs, 47–8
cracks, 44, 145
Crane, Walter, *129*
Crapper, Thomas, 80–1
crime, 98
Cruikshank, George, *9*, 26, 101–2, *101*
Crystal Palace, *27*, 28, 80, 116
Cubitt, Thomas, 35
curtains, 62–3, *62, 125*

damp, 136
    causes, 145
    in cellars, 36–7
    mortar and, 41
    rising damp, 137, 145
    valley gutter roofs, 50
damp-proof course (DPC), 137, 145
Day, Lewis F., 69, 70
death rates, 105, 132
deflection, walls, 44
Delamotte, *27*
Department of the Environment, 143
Deptford, 12
The Diary of a Nobody, 8, 57, 104–5, 119
Dickens, Charles, 23, 98
dining rooms, 62, 69, *71, 73*
directories, trade, 155–7
disease, 97–8
distemper, 94
doors, 145
Doré, Gustave, *14*
double-glazing, 53, 136
drainpipes, 50
draughtproofing, 136–7
drawing rooms, 69, *72*
dressing rooms, 58–9, 82
drinking, 100–2, 109
drinking fountains, *108*, 109
dry rot, 42, 55, 145
Du Maurier, George, *29*
Dyos, H.J., 35

Earls Court, *36*
Eastlake, Charles, 45, 57, 70–1, *72–3*, 76, 128
Edis, Robert W., *74*, 75
education, 100
Edward, Prince of Wales (*later* Edward VII),
    80
electric lighting, 90

employment:
    apprenticeships, 35
    servants, 25–6, *25, 26*
    in slums, 25
Enfield, 11
English and Welsh House Condition Surveys,
    147
Enveloping Schemes, 151
Erddig, *118*
estate agents, 142–3
estates, 101–4
    philanthropic, 24, *24*, 63
Euston Station, *13*, 14
extensions, 82, 137–9
Ferrabee, John, 114
finance:
    grants, 149–52
    mortgages, 35, 143
    spec builders, 35–6
fireplaces, 60, *74, 86*, 87, 89, 120, 124
fires, coal, 86–7, 120, 124
Flemish bond, brickwork, 41–2
foundations, 37–8, 44, 47, 138, 145
fountains, drinking, *108*, 109
frost damage, 38
funerals, 105
furniture, 127–8

garden furniture, *113*, 114, 117
The Gardener's Magazine, 114–16
gardens, 110–19
gas lighting, 90, *96*
General Improvement Areas, 151
General Register Office, 158
George V, King, *160*
Germany, 81
geysers, 84, *84*
Gissing, George, 57, 69
glass, 26–8
    conservatories, *111, 112*, 116
    opaque, *88*, 89
    see also windows
glasshouses, *111*, 112–13
Gothic Revival, 41, 94, *148*
graining, paintwork, 89, 91
grants, 149-52
graveyards, 105–6, *106, 107*
Great Exhibition (1851), 28, 80, 116
Greater London Council (GLC), 161
Grossmith, George and Weedon, *The Diary of
    a Nobody, 8*, 57, 104–5, 119
The Guardian, 98
guilds, 34–5
gutters, 48–50

Hackney Marshes, 38
halls, *62*, 63, *64*
handrails, staircases, 55
Harrow, *40*
Haweis, Mrs, 68, 69, 76

heating, 136
    central heating, 86, *86*, 125
    coal fires, 86–7, 120, 124
    water, 83–4, *84*
Highgate Cemetery, *106, 107*
Historic Buildings Company, 143
House Hospital, Battersea, 124
housekeepers, 130–1, *131*
housework, 25–6, *25*, 59–60, 130–2
Housing Action Areas (HAA), 151
housing associations, 151–2
housing standards, legislation, 28–31
Huguenots, 157
Humpherson, Frederick, 80–1, *81*, 82
Humphries, Steve, 76–7

Imperial Gas, Light and Coke Company, 104
improvement grants, 149–50, 151
incandescent lighting, 90, *90*
industrial revolution, 9–11, 23, 87
infill buildings, *150*
insect infestations, 55
Institute of Health Officers, 136
insulation, 136–7
insurance, 140–2
interior decorators, 69–71
intermediate grants, 149–50
Irish immigrants, *44*
ironwork, *48*
    railings, 92–4
Isham, Sir Charles, 116–17

Jacobean style, 75–6
Japanese influences, 72
Jekyll, Gertrude, 117–18
Jennings, George, 80, *83*
jerry-building, 32
joists, 42, 44, 47

Kentish Town, 163–4
Kershaw, 89
keystones, *144*
kingposts, 48
Kings Cross Station, 14
kitchen gardens, 118–19
kitchens, 59, 132–5, *133*

Ladies' Lavatory Company, 77
The Lady, 64–5
Lambton, Lucinda, 106
landowners, 22
lath and plaster walls, 44–5
lavatories, 77, 80–2, *81*
lawnmowers, 113–14
lawns, 113–14
legislation, housing standards, 28–31
Liberty's, *90*
libraries, 155, 158, 161, 163
lighting, 90–1, *91*, 124
Linley Sambourne House, *46*, 50, *64*, 65–6, 89,

110, *110*, 121, 123, 124, *125*
listed buildings, 151, 152
Liverpool, 32, 40, 73, 109
Local Government Board, 29
loft extensions, 137–8
lofts, 50, 147
London:
    Bartholomew Lane, 100
    Belgrave Square, *10*
    Bucknall Street, 15
    Church Lane, 15–16, *15*
    Dragon Road, 35
    Farringdon Road, 98
    Farringdon Street, 19
    Hatton Garden, 157
    housing legislation, 29
    Kennington Gate Turnpike, *17*
    New Oxford Street, 15–16
    Oxford Street, 77, 98–100
    parks, 109
    Pear Tree Court, *97*, 98
    sewers, 80
    shops, 76–7
    Stafford Terrace, *49*, 123
    Tottenham Court Road, 104
    tracing history of houses, 155–61
    Trafalgar Square, 109
    transport, 11–21
    watertable, 37, 40
    Whitehorse Lane, 19
    see also individual districts and suburbs
London Bridge Station, 12, 14
London and Greenwich Railway Company, 12
London stock bricks, 41
London Tramways, 20
Loudon, John Claudius, 82, 86, 106, 114, 116
Loudon, Mrs, 69, 116
Lowcock, Charles Frederick, *59*, *70*

McIntosh, Charles, 114, 116
Maughan's Patent Geyser, *84*
Manchester, 28
Manchester University, 163
Mansfield, John M., 127
mantelpieces, *74*
Maple & Co., *62*
maps, 161–3
marbling, 89, 91
Martin, Paul, *158, 159, 164*
Mary, Queen (Consort of George V), *160*
Mason, Walter E., 82
Metropolitan Board of Works, 80
Metropolitan Commission for Sewers, 80
Mills, John Fitzmaurice, 127
monuments, 109
morning rooms, *61*, 62
Morris, William, *121, 129*
mortar, 40–1
mortgages, 35, 143

'nail sickness', 144
National Library of Wales, 161
Nelson's Column, 109
Neo-Gothic, 72
New Landscape School, 118
New Scientist, 40
New York, 94, 109
newspapers, research, 161
Nield, Ted, 40
nursemaids, 131–2

Oakbank House, Perth, 160, 164
omnibuses, 16–17, *16*, *19*
Operative Bricklayers' Society, *33*
Ordnance Survey, 161

Paddington, 19
Paddington Station, 14
paintings, 69, 72–3
paints and paintworks, 89, 145
    graining, 89, 91
    marbling, 89, 91
    paints, 94–5
    railings, 92–4
    stucco, 95–6
    window frames, 94, 95, *95*
Palace of Westminster, 94
Panton, Mrs, 36–7, 57, 67–9, 71, 72, 76, 86
parapets, 50
Paris, 94
Paris Exhibition, 89
parks, 109–10, 113, *117*, *162*
parlours, 60, 62, 63–5, 69
party walls, 43–4
pattern books, 28, 71, 72
Paxton, Sir Joseph, 28, 109, 116
Peabody estates, 24, *24*, *97*, 98
Peckham, 17
Penge, 11
The Period Property Register, 143
Perth, 159–60, 164
Peter Robinson's, 76
philanthropic housing estates, 24, *24*, 63
Picturesque, 114
Pidgeon, Geoffrey, 82
pitched roofs, 47–8
Planning Permission, 152–4
plaster:
    lath and plaster walls, 44–5
    plasterwork, 89
    stucco, 45–7, *46*
plumbing, 82–3
pollution, 86–7, *87*, 136
portraits, 72–3
public conveniences, 80
Public Health Acts, 28–9, 80
Public Record Office, 161
pubs, *88*, *101*, 102
Pugin, A.W., 94
Punch, *29*, *32*, *78*

Quarterly Review, 75
queenposts, 45, 48

rafters, 47, 48
railings, 92–4, *142*
railways, 11–15, 16, 20–1, 26, 161–3
ratebooks, 159–60
rear extensions, 82, 137, 138
red builders (bricks), 41
Red House, Bexleyheath, *121*
Regents Park, 109
rented accommodation, 21, 35, 57, 58
repair grants, 149–50
Riden, Philip, 163
rising damp, 137, 145
road surfaces, 98–100
Robinson, John Martin, 120
Robinson, William, 118
roofs, 47–50
    butterfly, 48–50
    flat, 138
    maintenance, 145–7
    pitched, 47–8
    replacing, 47
    ridged, 47–8
    supports, 45
    understructured, 47, 144
    valley gutters, 48–50
rookeries, 15–16, 23, 29, 78, 97–8
rubbers (bricks), 41
rugs, 75
Rumford, Count, 87

St John's Wood, *30*
St Sepulchre, Snow Hill, 105
sanitation, 28–9, 77–82
sash cords, replacing, 52–3
scaffolding, 140, *141*
Science Museum, London, 83, 134
Scotland, 159–60
Scott, Benjamin, 109
Second World War, 38
servants, 21, 25–6, *25*, 58–60, 82, 123, 129-32, *131*
The Servant's Practical Guide, 62
Severs, Dennis, 124
sewage, 78–81
sewer records, 161
sewers, 40, 78–80, *79*
Shelter, 149
Shillibeer, George, 16–17, 19
Shoolbred's, *72*, 76, 104
shops, 76–7, *102*, *103*, *104*
skylights, 138
slates, 28, 47, 144, 147
slums, 15–16, 21, 23, 25, 29, 78, 97–8
Soane, Sir John, 120
Society for Improving the Condition of the Labouring Classes, 24
Solo Park, Cambridgeshire, 124

Solomon, Solomon Joseph, *67*
Sparrow, V. Shaw, 63
speculative builders, 22–3, 28, 31, 35–6
spine walls, 44
Spitalfields, 124
Staffordshire blue bricks, 41
stairs, 55–6, *62*
statuary, garden, 116
Stead, David, 98
stock bricks, 41
Stoke Newington, 38, 104, 163
stone-effect cladding, *150*, 154
street sweepers, 78
stucco, 45–7, *46*, 95–6
stud walls, 44–5
studies, *68*, *74*
subsidence, 44, 145
suburbs, 11
summer houses, *113*, 118
surveys, 144–5
Sydenham, *27*

Tay, River, 164
terraced houses, 42–3, *43*, 56, *150*
Thames, River, 12, 80
Thornton Heath, 19
tie bars, 42, *43*, 145
tie beams, 47
tiles, roof, 47
timber:
    rotten, 55, 145
    roofs, 47
    timber pile foundations, 38
    woodworm, 55
The Times, 17
Tindall, Gillian, 21–2, 163
Tithe Commutation Act (1836), 161
tithe maps, 161
title deeds, 155
Tonna, Charlotte Elizabeth, 105
Totterdown Estate, Tooting, *160*
trade directories, 155–7
traffic, 98, *99*
Train, George Francis, *18*, 19
trams, *18*, 19–20
transport:
    buses, 17
    omnibuses, 16–17, *16*, *19*
    railways, 11–15, 16, 20–1
    trams, *18*, 19–20
    underground railways, *18*, 19
Tudor style, 72, 75–6
Twyford, *81*
typhoid, 80

underground railways, *18*, 19
urea-formaldehyde foam insulation, 137
urinals, 82

vacuum cleaners, *133*, 134
Vaughan Library, Harrow, *40*
valuation rolls, 159–60
ventilation, 89, 136–7
Victoria, Queen, 65
Victoria and Albert Museum, London, 89, 92
Victoria Park, London, *108*
Victoria Station, *20*
Victorian Society, *46*, 50, 121

Walker, Dr, 105
wallpaper, 66, *129*
    removing, 45
walls:
    cavity walls, 138
    cracks, 44, 145
    deflection, 44
    internal, 44–5
    party walls, 43–4
    removing, 44–5, 60
    spine walls, 44
    strength, 42
    see also bricks and brickwork
Ward, Dr Nathaniel Bagshaw, 110–11
Wardian cases, 110–12, *110*, 113
water, heating, 83–4, *84*
watertable, 37, 38–40
Watson, Mrs, 69
Weightman, Gavin, 76–7
Wellington, Duke of, 92
West Ham, 21
wet rot, 145
Whiteley's, *77*
Willesden, 21
window tax, 26–8
windows, 50–5, *138*
    bay, *54*, 54–5
    casement, 53–4
    curtains, 62–3, *62*
    dormers, 50, 137
    double-glazing, 53, 136
    frames, 94, 95, *95*
    roof, 138
    sash, 52–4
    timbers, 145
Witton, Birmingham, 40
woodworm, 55

Yates, Edward, 35, 36

Zinsser, Hans, 97